A BRIEF HISTORY OF
ENGLISH BIBLE TRANSLATIONS

Other titles available by Laurence M. Vance:
The Other Side of Calvinism

A BRIEF HISTORY OF ENGLISH BIBLE TRANSLATIONS

by

Laurence M. Vance, B.D., Th.M., Th.D.

Vance Publications
Pensacola, FL

ISBN 0-9628898-1-4
Library of Congress Catalog Card Number: 93-93831

Published and Distributed by: Vance Publications
P.O. Box 11781, Pensacola, FL 32524, 904-474-1626

Printed by: Rose Printing Company
Tallahassee, FL

TABLE OF CONTENTS

PREFACE

Is the Bible the word of God? In previous decades, this question concerned the conservative declaration that the Bible was the verbally inspired, authoritative word of God. This affirmation was in opposition to the liberal position that the Bible only contained the word of God and the neo-orthodox view that the Bible merely becomes the word of God. Although this debate still rages in some circles, it is not the occupation of this endeavor.

With the ongoing proliferation of English translations of the Bible, the question at hand takes on an entirely new meaning. The doctrine of the inspiration and authority of the Bible being presupposed, the query now becomes: Which Bible is the word of God? The alarming propensity at which each new translation finds acceptance among one group or another has even given rise to "specialty" versions which have been adapted to the assorted theological persuasions, lifestyles, and presuppositions of the reader. Aside from the obvious proclivity toward the corruption and misappropriation of the word of God, this practice further renders it necessary to not only inquire, but to ascertain which Bible or Bibles constitute the word of God.

Upon surveying the existing supply of available English Bible translations, and observing the continuing multiplication of new ones, it was deemed both desirous and necessary to compile a list of the various translations together with their respective date of appearance. This index now gives way to a more complete, accurate, and annotated catalog of translations tracing the origin and development of English Bible translations from before the invention of printing to the present day.

The approach to this undertaking will necessarily be *brief.* More has been written about all the various aspects of the Bible than any other book or books. The concentrated effort will be on *history* and information, not analysis and indictment. Neither the relative merits and demerits of the various English translations, nor the character and motives of the translators, will be under immediate consideration. Our chief concern is the *English* Bible, both by sheer magnitude of number and its unprovincial nature. There are more translations of the Bible in the universal language of the world than all the major languages combined. It is only complete *Bible* translations that are critical to this study. An incalculable number of translations of individual books of the Bible are neither pertinent nor advantageous to the stated goal of this venture. It is only initial English Bible *translations* that warrant our attention: the multitude of editions and styles of the various versions is inconsequential.

Although this treatise will not directly concern itself with the authorship, history and constitution of the various Greek and Hebrew texts, a brief survey of the formation and establishment of their printed editions will be made because it is deemed relevant to the purpose of the work, since they form the primary foundation upon which all translations are based. However, textual criticism, extant manuscripts, papyrus fragments, and ancient versions, along with Greek grammar, Hebrew syntax, and the conjectures and emendations of the scholars, are markedly impertinent to the task at hand. The relevance and importance of these matters have been prodigiously debated and will continue to be so.

Respecting the accuracy of all historical statements contained herein, the utmost consideration will be made of respected sources and all assertions should be deemed factual and authentic. However, the older and more unrenowned a particular translation is, the less certitude can be expected with respect to some details; other detriments to accuracy and the determining methods employed being more fully chronicled in the Introduction. Likewise, the fact of antiquity, coupled with the vast number of translations found throughout history, renders some omissions inevitable. It is also admitted that in the treatment of recent versions, by its very nature, a work such as this is rendered somewhat obsolete with the passage of time and certain release of future English translations.

INTRODUCTION

The history of English translations of the Bible is a long and often controversial one. In the beginning, the objection was not to the character and constitution of the translation or the motive and methods of the translators, but to the actual fact of the existence of an unauthorized, vernacular translation of the Bible in English. In contrast, the predicament at the present time is not one of availability and acceptance, but of abundance and saturation.

By the time translations first appeared in the English language, the Bible had already been widely copied and circulated for hundreds of years in many different forms. Copies of portions of the Old Testament, which was originally written in Hebrew, were usually in the form of a scroll that would be unwound for reading. These scrolls were initially made from leather, and later from papyrus and vellum or parchment. The invention of the book-like codex provided another element to copy the Scriptures on. There are extant manuscripts in Hebrew both of the scroll and codex. The oldest known manuscript of the entire Hebrew Old Testament is the Leningrad Codex from about the year 1000.

Since it came later in time, the New Testament, which was originally written in Greek, is to be found copied extensively in codices. Most of these were constructed from papyrus. The extant manuscripts of the Greek New Testament, from which a text is established, consist of several types. Majuscules or uncials were written in block capital letters while minuscules or cursives approximate smaller cursive script. The papyri are papyrus fragments that may contain entire books or only a few verses. In addition to these types of manuscripts, which number more than 3000, there are three other witnesses to the text of the

New Testament. Lectionaries are books that contain selected passages of Scripture designed to be used in public church services throughout the year. Patristic citations are scriptural quotations included in the commentaries, sermons, and other writings of the Church Fathers. The final witness to the text of the New Testament is ancient versions, which are nothing more than translations of the Bible from Greek into other languages including Coptic, Armenian, Georgian, Ethiopic, Gothic, Latin, Syriac, and Slavonic.

Not only was the Bible not initially written in English, the original manuscripts were not at first put together into one book. The word *bible* comes from the Latin word *biblia*, which is a singular word. This in turn came to us from the Greek word *biblia*, which is not a singular word but a plural, signifying *books*, and more specifically, the sixty-six books of what we call the Bible. The plural *biblia* is really a diminutive form of *biblos*, which is what papyrus or bublus was called when it was made into a useable form from the bublos plant. This reed, which grew plentifully in the Nile, was cut into thin strips and fastened together to produce a sheet or roll. The plant derived its name from the ancient Phoenician town of Gebal that was called Bublos by the Greeks because it was the port through which papyrus came from Egypt. It is to be remembered that the alphabet is Phoenician in origin, which would explain the need for paper: to write on. So *ta biblia*, "the books," had to be put together as one. This was termed the canon, from *kanon*, originally meaning a reed or rod, then a measuring rod, and finally a rule or standard.

With the necessary materials available for the construction of the Hebrew and Greek texts, and the canon of Scripture being already decided, the actual formation and establishment of the biblical texts and their subsequent translation into the English Bible was ready to begin. It is here that we commence our historical examination, with only brief attention given to the period before.

There are several notable works that undertake to provide an exhaustive history of English Bible translations. The trouble is that their size and magnitude, together with their unavailability and expense, render them arduous to obtain. They are also usually somewhat antiquated and hence fail to adequately treat relatively modern translations. On the other end of the spectrum, there are readily obtainable publications that merely provide an analysis of a select few English versions. In between, we have treatments of the English Bible that are part of larger works on Bible manuscripts, Bible history, or ancient versions. These works are by their very nature inadequate for the pursuit of an exhaustive account of English Bible translations. Other works of singular purpose are likewise incomplete because of an emphasis on major translations or certain time periods. Exclusive issues of papers or articles are of negligible value due to their limited circulation. Not that all of this material is not useful. It is the fact that all this material is required to reach a conclusion that this work has been undertaken.

The intention of this labor has been stated as to trace the origin and development of English Bible translations from before the invention of printing to the present day. It is the history and composition and not the motive and accuracy of these English Bible translations that is our primary concern. Any conclusions drawn from this history will be treated in an epilogue. A brief synopsis of all modern translations is provided as well as an extended treatment of all essential and significant versions found throughout history: the disparity in the material regarding each translation being directly related to the importance and availability of information on each respective version. An appendix containing a comprehensive tabulation of all English translations of the Bible, both extant and extinct, will supplement the work. This task naturally divides itself into five periods:

1. The beginning to Tyndale
2. Tyndale to the Authorized Version
3. Authorized to the Revised Version
4. Revised Version to the Revised Standard Version
5. Revised Standard Version to the present

The inclusion in this work of any particular version depends on several factors. With but one or two exceptions, the focus of this work is on complete Bibles or separate Old or New

Testaments. Translations of selections or of single books of the Bible number in the hundreds. This is especially true of the Gospels, Epistles, and the Psalms. The arduous task of cataloging all these attempts at Bible translation remains to be attempted. Although many commentaries offer a new translation as part of their venture, only works actually offered as translations are under consideration. The simple reason being that it is not feasible and practically impossible to ascertain which biblical commentaries proffered a new translation. That is a subject all to itself. To be precise and equitable, each individual translation is included but one time. Where the Old or New Testament was issued first, the date and the information given is that of the publication of the entire Bible or the later Testament if no unified Bible was produced. The same holds true for Bibles or Testaments released in series over a period of years: the date of publication of the completed work is our foremost concern. Many translations, especially modern ones, are available in many different editions, formats, and styles, depending on the desired audience of the publishers. The initial, primary release of each translation is the basis of this work unless extensively revised and published as such. The only exception to this is when one translation is unsuspectingly marketed under another name. Unpublicized minor revisions to the text of all Bibles have occurred in subsequent printings.

Meticulous, painstaking accuracy has been striven for, especially in regard to determining exact dates out of the mass of sometimes conflicting evidences. Other hindrances to complete precision concern the proper name of some translations, particularly in regard to the word *the* at the beginning of the title of many modern versions. Regarding the more ancient translations, it is the correct spelling, punctuation, and capitalization of the title that is often in doubt. It is also sometimes difficult to ascertain whether a specific translation is really a whole Bible or just an Old or New Testament. Equally demanding is the task of resolving whether a certain Bible is actually another translation at all, and not just an edition, usually of the Authorized Version or the Douay Rheims, with notes and other additions. Another problem encountered is determining whether a series of translations of individual books of the Bible was ever finished and compiled into one Bible. Where these questions do arise, however, the judgment of the author must necessarily intervene. All the standard and authoritative sources have been used, with all direct quotes concerning modern translations taken directly from the Preface of the respective versions. Indeed, wherever possible, recourse was made directly to each version in question, and especially those contained in the author's personal collection of over 100 modern translations. Footnotes have been dispensed with to eliminate unnecessary clutter, since it is not the primary purpose of this work to bring to light heretofore unproven new knowledge, but to make old knowledge more accessible.

CHAPTER ONE

IN THE BEGINNING

The first attempt to translate the Bible directly from its original languages into English was a great distance removed from the completion and canonization of the Bible many hundred years previously. Before this landmark event could take place, however, there were many serious obstacles to be overcome. Although the Bible existed in England before this time, it was not an English Bible. The language of the church was for all practical purposes, Latin. And although that was a hindrance to the production of an English Bible, even more so was the fact that English as a language, for much of this period, did not even exist as we know it. What early English translations did exist, however, were never complete nor circulated. The first complete Bible, that of Wycliffe, antedated the invention of printing, therefore severely limiting its usefulness. The formation and establishment of the Hebrew and Greek texts from which to translate from had not yet occurred. It was only when all these barriers were removed that the history of the English Bible could unfold. The grave significance of the Reformation should also be stressed, but as that is a voluminous study in itself, it would be inappropriate to introduce it here.

The Latin Vulgate

Although the Old Testament was written in Hebrew and the New in Greek, the first English Bibles were translated, not from the Hebrew and Greek, but from the Latin, and in particular, the Latin Vulgate. Therefore, it is pertinent to compactly examine the role of the Latin Vulgate in relation to the history of English

Bible translations. The official language of the Roman Empire was Latin; the official church, the Roman Catholic Church. Both language and church continued together until the sixteenth century when the publication of the Bible in the vernacular tongues liberated the people from both. The New Testament was translated into Latin by the end of the second century, but it was the supposedly wide divergences that existed in the Old Latin, due to its manifold and dissimilar translation efforts, that led to a revision of the Old Latin by Jerome. According to Augustine:

> Those who translated the Scriptures from Hebrew into Greek can be counted, but the Latin translators are out of all number. For in the early days of the faith, every man who happened to gain possession of a Greek manuscript and who imagined he had any facility in both languages, however slight that might have been, dared to make a translation.

Jerome (346-420) was one of the most competent scholars of his day. He studied grammar and rhetoric at Rome, as well as Greek language and literature, and afterward learned Hebrew. He travelled extensively and later translated some of the works of Origen. He wrote several biblical commentaries, but his prominent achievement was his translation of the Bible into Latin. In 382, Pope Damasus summoned Jerome from Constantinople to Rome and commissioned him to revise the Old Latin to produce an authoritative edition of the Latin Bible that would supersede it. Jerome later wrote in his Preface:

> You urge me to revise the Old Latin version, and, as it were, to sit in judgement on the copies of the Scriptures which are now scattered throughout the world; and, inasmuch as they differ from one another, you would have me decide which of them agree with the Greek original.

The Gospels were completed in 384 and the rest of the New Testament soon followed. Pope Damasus then died and Jerome left Rome, finally settling in Bethlehem. Here he began a private venture of translating and revising the Old Testament on the basis of the Septuagint. Jerome then abandoned the Greek Old Testament and went directly to the Hebrew. He issued his translation in segments during the years 390 to 404. His resulting translation existed side by side with the Old Latin for centuries before it became universally adopted. The designation of his work as the Latin Vulgate was not regularly applied before the thirteenth century for even the Old Latin at the time of Jerome was even called the *editio vulgate,* the common edition. It was in the Vulgate that current chapter divisions, accredited to Stephen Langton (d.1228), were first introduced into the Bible.

There are no complete Old Latin manuscripts of the Old or New Testaments in existence today. Whereas all of the manuscripts of the Old Latin are extant only in fragments, there are countless numbers of Vulgate manuscripts scattered throughout the world. The Vulgate went through numerous revisions and editions during its history. In 1546, the Council of Trent decreed the Vulgate "only of all other Latin translations to be authentical," and required that it be printed as much as possible without errors. In 1585, Pope Sixtus V sought to revise and correct the Vulgate to prepare an authentic edition. It was completed in 1590 and called the Sixtine Bible. Two years later, Pope Clement VIII stopped circulation of his predecessor's edition and issued his own authentic edition. This Clementine Vulgate, as it was called, remains the official Latin Bible of the Roman Catholic Church today.

The English Language

The English language is part of the Anglo-Frisian group within the western branch of the Germanic languages. It is an extensive, influential, living and growing language made up of an estimated one million words, with constant editions each year. Prolonged and comprehensive borrowing from every major language and numerous minor languages accounts for this great vocabulary. English is truly the universal language. Between 1600 and the present, the speakers of English, through armies, companies, relocation, and expeditions, carried their language and culture into all corners of the globe. It is the language of technology and science, business and commerce, news and information, mail and communications, and Christianity. Not only is English the native language for millions of people, it is also a competing second language, a unifying alternative language, or a viable foreign language for millions more. Whatever the total number of speakers are, English, at the end of the twentieth century, is more widely distributed, spoken, and written than any other language has ever been. Consequently, there are more English translations of the Bible than all the major languages combined. In contrast to English, Latin is now classified as a dead language.

The remarkable thing about the English language is that it is not altogether native to England. The real history of England begins, not with prehistoric times, but with the invasions of the Angles, Saxons, and Jutes who sailed across the North Sea in the fifth century. The native Britons were dispossessed, and seven kingdoms were eventually set up roughly corresponding to present-day England. The Germanic conquerors of Britain are collectively referred to as Anglo-Saxons. To the Britons they were *Angelcynn* and their language was *Englisc*. Bede's Church History of England, written in Latin, was called the *Historia Ecclesiastica Gentis Anglorum*. By about 1000 A.D., the land of the *Angles* was generally known as *Englaland*. It is practically impossible to write a modern English sentence without drawing from Anglo-Saxon or Old English.

These seven kingdoms of England were united in 829 by King Egbert of Wessex of the kingdom of the Saxons. The Danish Conquest began at the end of the eighth century with the Norsemen or Danes from Scandinavia conquering northern France (Normandy) and invading England. By 871, most of northern England was subject to the foreign invaders. Alfred the Great (849-901), who acceded the throne in 871, stopped the Danes and they withdrew to the north. King Alfred arranged to have many Latin books translated into English and instituted the compilation of the *Anglo-Saxon Chronicle*, valuable as an early history of England. New Danish invasions came at the beginning of the eleventh century and in 1016 King Cnut of Denmark inherited the English throne, conquered Norway and completed the Danish conquest. The Danish settlers had a profound influence on the development of Old English. There are about 900 words in the English language of Scandinavian origin. Many Latin words, a number of which were derived from Greek, were also introduced during the Old English period of our language.

The next period in the development of the English language, appropriately called Middle English, extends from the Norman Conquest in 1066 to about 1500. William the Conqueror, Duke of Normandy, had his coronation in Westminster Abbey on Christmas Day of 1066. Norman bishops and clergyman gradually assumed positions in the churches. All important posts in the country were controlled by French-speaking Normans. French was established as the social and cultural language while Latin remained the primary language of learning and religion. The surviving English vernacular was the speech of the common man. This period was one of continued developments in the English language. Words were naturally introduced from the French and many changes in accidence and pronunciation occurred. War with France naturally brought about a revival of the English tongue, and Henry V (1387-1422) was the first king since the Norman Conquest to use English for his official correspondence.

The modern period of the English language coincides with the invention of printing, the Renaissance, the Reformation, the rise of England as a maritime power, and the translation of the Bible from the original languages into English. The single most influential book ever produced in the English language, the Authorized Version of the Bible in 1611, remains the supreme, crowning achievement in English literature.

Early English Translations

The history of the early English translations of the Bible is not only somewhat obscure, it is indefinite and relatively unknown. In England, as in other countries, the people became familiar with the Bible in their own language through hearing not reading. The first presumed attempt to translate a portion of the Bible into English was the Paraphrases of Caedmon (d.680), whose poetic songs paraphrased portions of Scripture into Anglo-Saxon. Aldhelm (604-709) and Guthlac (d.794) were both thought to have translated the Psalms. About this same time, Egbert allegedly translated the Gospels also. The Venerable Bede (673-735), a renowned scholar who wrote an ecclesiastical history as well as a number of commentaries on the various books of the Bible, is thought to have translated part of the Gospel of John just before he died. Alfred the Great (849-901) translated some historical works and prefixed a translation of the Ten Commandments and other portions of Scripture to his code of laws. He was also thought to have been instrumental in a translation of the Psalter. The Lindisfarne Gospels is an interlinear gloss in Anglo-Saxon by Aldred (c.950) of a Latin version of the Gospels drafted by Eadfrith (d.721), bishop of Lindisfarne. Aelfric (955-1020) translated into Anglo-Saxon the first seven books of the Bible as well as some others. The Wessex Gospels and the Rushworth Gospels also originate from this period.

When we pass from Old to Middle English we find Orm (c.1215) paraphrasing selections from the Gospels and Acts into a work called the *Ormulum.* During the early part of the fourteenth century, three notable English Psalters appeared: the Surtees, the Rolle, and the West Midlands, attributed to William of Shoreham. Very few of these aforementioned attempts at translating the Bible into English are extant, but the work of a man born in the early part of the fourteenth century certainly is.

The Wycliffe Bible

John Wycliffe (c.1320-1384) is credited with being the first to translate the entire Bible into English. Assertions to the contrary have never been decisively proved, for although the exact history of Wycliffe and his Bible is somewhat uncertain, knowledge about the period before him is vague and indefinite. It is to be remembered that no Greek or Hebrew texts, versions, or editions were yet fabricated. Wycliffe did his translating primarily from the only Bible then in use: the Latin Vulgate. Wycliffe was educated at Oxford and later became rector at Lutterworth, in Leicestershire. He is often called the "Morning Star of the Reformation" for his opposition to ecclesiastical abuses and the Papacy. He advocated the superiority of Scripture to the Pope, the Church, the Fathers, and all opinions of men. For hundreds of years, the Bible had been withheld from all but the clergy. Wycliffe considered this a cardinal error and sought to get the Bible into the hands of the common people. His New Testament translation was completed in 1380, and the entire Bible in 1382. It is not definitely known who assisted him other than Nicholas Hereford, who translated much of the Old Testament. John Purvey (c.1353-1428), one of Wycliffe's associates, is recognized as the editor to a revised edition of Wycliffe's Bible in 1388. The revision soon supplanted the original and demand outstripped supply, since printing was still unknown.

The influence of Wycliffe can be seen in the infamous "Constitutions of Oxford," which in 1408 forbade vulgar translations of the Bible and mentioned Wycliffe in doing so:

> We therefore enact and ordain that no one henceforth on his own authority translate any text of Holy Scripture into the English or other language, by way of a book, pamphlet, or tract, and that no book, pamphlet, or tract of this kind be read, either already recently composed in the time of the said John Wyclif, or since then, or that may in future be composed, in part or in whole, publicly or privily, under pain of the greater excommunication, until the translation itself shall have been approved by the diocesan of the place or if need be by a provincial council. Whoever shall do the contrary to be punished in like manner as a supporter of heresy and error.

In 1428, Wycliffe was posthumously condemned for heresy. His body was ceremoniously dug up, burned, and the ashes were scattered.

With the advent of printing, and English Bible translations beginning with Tyndale that were taken directly from the original languages, Wycliffe's Bible was gradually displaced and superseded. It was not until 1731 that Wycliffe's New Testament, in the revised form, was printed. The original version was published in 1848 and the entire Bible, in both versions, was published in 1850:

The Holy Bible, containing the Old and New Testaments, with the Apocryphal Books, in the earliest Versions made from the Latin Vulgate by John Wycliffe and his followers: edited by the Rev. Josiah Forshall, F.R.S. etc. and Sir Frederick Madden, K.H., F.R.S., etc, Oxford, at the University Press, 1850. Four volumes.

There are at present about 170 extant copies of Wycliffe's versions with most being the form of the revision.

The Printed Bible

For Wycliffe, or anyone else in his time, to translate the Bible was certainly quite remarkable, but as each copy had to be copied by hand, the time involved and the cost impeded wide circulation, not to mention the penchant for errors. The invention of printing, although primitive by modern standards, immediately remedied these problems. A multitude of copies could be made in a relatively short period of time without the preponderance of errors introduced through the inevitable corruption of copies by human error.

The acknowledged inventor of printing is John Gutenberg of Mainz, Germany. Like Wycliffe, the whole story of Gutenberg and his printing press is obscure. The first major work thought to appear from his presses was the Bible, finished in 1456. This edition of the Latin Vulgate is often called the "Gutenberg Bible," and about forty copies are known to exist in the world today. Before 1500, the total number of books printed throughout Europe was about 35,000, and most of those in Latin. By 1640, some 20,000 different items were thought to have been printed in English alone.

Although printing was introduced in England about the year 1476 by William Caxton, the earliest printed vernacular Bibles were those of the chief languages of Europe: a German Bible was printed at Strassburg in 1466; an Italian Bible at Venice in 1471; Dutch and French Bibles followed respectively in 1477 and 1487; a Portuguese translation was printed in 1495. In 1477, the entire Hebrew Old Testament was first printed; the complete

Old Testament with vowels points and accents was issued in 1488. Greek was first publicly taught in 1458 at Paris, and although a grammar was published in 1476 and a lexicon in 1480, the only biblical Greek printed before the sixteenth century were editions of the Psalter. But it would not be long before the first printed edition of the Greek New Testament would appear that gave impetus to the first English translation taken directly from the Greek.

CHAPTER TWO

THE GOLDEN AGE

The next period of major concern in the history of English Bible translations is from the very first Bible translated into English directly from the original languages, that of William Tyndale in 1525, to the capstone of this era, the Authorized Version of 1611. This golden age of English Bible translations closely parallels that of the formation of the text of the Old and New Testaments. And rightly so, for in order to have a translation, one must have something to translate from. Until this time, the only thing available was the Latin Vulgate, and that not readily, since printing was unknown. But with the invention of printing came the ability to circulate printed copies of the text of the Scriptures in Hebrew and Greek, and thus facilitate translation. Thus it is also pertinent to examine the formation and establishment of the Hebrew and Greek texts underlying the Bibles of this period, since they are the primary foundation upon which all translations are based.

The Hebrew Old Testament

The first Rabbinic Hebrew Bible with full vowel-points, accents, Targum, and commentary was published by Daniel Bomberg at Venice in 1516-17. This was the first Hebrew text to divide the books of Samuel, Kings, and Chronicles into two books. The second edition of this work, edited by Jacob ben Chayyim, appeared in 1524-25. This became the standard and authoritative edition of the Masoretic Text until the third edition of Kittel's *Biblia Hebraica* in 1937. The first edition of the Hebrew text to be published under direction and authority of Christians appeared in the Complutensian Polyglot.

The Greek New Testament

To the Complutensian Polyglot (so called because it was published at Alcala, Spain, the Latin form of which is Complutum), which was prepared by Cardinal Ximenes (d.1517), also belongs the distinction of being the first printed edition of the Greek New Testament. The New Testament, containing the Greek text on the left and a Latin translation on the right, was finished in 1514. The Old Testament, adding a third column in Hebrew, was completed in 1517. However, the entire work was not actually published and made available until 1522. Other polyglots appeared later, most notably, the Antwerp (1569-72), the Paris (1629-45), and the London (1655-57).

The first circulated edition of the Greek New testament, though printed later than the work of Ximenes, was published earlier. It was the work of Desiderius Erasmus (1469-1536), who stated: "I vehemently dissent from those who would not have private persons read the Holy Scriptures, nor have them translated into the vulgar tongues." The first edition appeared in 1516 with a Latin translation in a parallel column. The second edition of 1519 corrected numerous printing errors and was the basis of the German translation of Martin Luther (1483-1546). In 1522, a third edition appeared in which he introduced the Johannine Comma. This edition became the basis for the later standardized text. For the fourth edition of 1527, Erasmus made use of the Complutensian Polyglot and added the Vulgate in a third column. The fifth and final edition appeared in 1535.

In 1534, Simon de Colines (Colinaeus) published an edition of the Greek New Testament based in part on Erasmus and the Complutensian Polyglot, although he used additional manuscripts. This version had no influence on later editions.

Robert Estienne (1503-1559), better known as Stephanus, was the stepson of Colinaeus. He published several more editions of the Greek New Testament beginning in 1546. A similar second edition appeared in 1549. The third edition in 1550 had the distinction of being the first Greek New Testament with a critical apparatus and was the standard text in England until the time of the Revised Version. A fourth edition was issued at Geneva in 1551 which included Erasmus' Latin version and the Vulgate. This was the first Bible of any kind to contain the modern verse divisions.

The next editor of the New Testament in Greek was Theodore Beza (1519-1605). His Greek New Testament went through ten editions. Only four of them, however, were independent editions (1565, 1582, 1589, 1598). These editions included the Latin Vulgate as well as Beza's own Latin translation. In the preparation of his text, Beza relied upon the text of Stephanus with the notes and collations of his son Henry, patristic evidence, and several manuscripts he collated himself, including two of his own, Codex Bezae and Codex Claromontanus. The text he printed differs little from the work of Stephanus. His editions of 1589 and 1598 were used ostensively by the King James translators.

The final editions of the Greek New Testament in this period of the establishment of the Received Text were the seven editions of the Elzevir partners, Bonaventure and Abraham, published between 1624 and 1678. They were based largely upon the works of Stephanus and Beza. It is the second edition (1633) which declared that this was the text received by all and free from alteration or corruption, and which the designation "textus receptus" comes from: *"Textum ergo habes, nunc ab omnibus receptum: in quo nihil immutatum aut corruptum damus."*

The Tyndale Bible

William Tyndale (c.1494-1536) has the distinction of being the first to translate the New Testament from Greek into English. He early distinguished himself as a scholar both at Cambridge and Oxford, and was fluent in several languages. Tyndale soon advanced both his desire and his demise, as seen in his reply to a critic: "I defy the pope and all his laws; if God spare my life, ere many years I will cause the boy that driveth the plough in England to know more of the Scriptures than thou doest." The Bible was still forbidden in the vernacular so after settling in London for several months while attempting to gain approval for his translation efforts, Tyndale concluded: "Not only that there was no room in my lord of Londons palace to translate the New Testament, but also that there was no place to do it in all England, as experience doth now openly declare."

Accordingly, Tyndale left England in 1524 and completed his translation of the New Testament in Hamburg and Wittenberg. Unlike modern scholars, Tyndale had no technical help like the multitude of grammars, lexicons, manuscripts, texts, and versions available today. He used primarily the third edition of Erasmus and had available Luther's German, the Latin Vulgate, and conceivably, the Complutensian Polyglot. The moving factor in his translation of the New Testament was that he "perceived by experience, how that it was impossible to establish the lay people in any truth, except the scripture were plainly laid before their eyes in their mother tongue, that they might see the process, order and meaning of the text."

In 1525, he removed to Cologne to have his work printed. The printer, Peter Quentel, had his work stopped after printing ten sheets. Tyndale secured the printed sheets, which contained the Prologue, the Gospel of Matthew, and part of Mark. Arriving in Worms, he finished not only the partly printed edition, but another as well. Both editions were finished late in 1525 and shortly thereafter were smuggled into England. The book was an instant success, and in spite of all efforts to the contrary, copies continued to pour into England as fast as they were purchased or destroyed. The ecclesiastical authorities bought up all the obtainable copies from the printers, but this only enabled Tyndale to bring himself out of debt and revise and print his New Testament once more.

Tyndale then turned his attention to the Old Testament. The Pentateuch was published in 1530 and the book of Jonah in 1531. In 1534, a revised edition of the New Testament and the Pentateuch appeared. Further revisions of the New Testament were issued in 1535. The order of biblical books follows Luther in putting Hebrews, James, Jude, and the Revelation as the last four books in the New Testament. Although chapter divisions were used, the text was not divided into verses. On May 21, 1535, Tyndale was treacherously kidnapped and imprisoned in Belgium. While in prison, he translated Joshua to 2 Chronicles. On October 6, 1536, Tyndale was tried as a heretic and condemned to death. He was strangled and burned, but not before he uttered the immortal prayer of "Lord, open the King of England's eyes."

The Coverdale Bible

Although Tyndale's English Bible was the first to be translated directly from the original languages, it was just the New Testament. It was Myles Coverdale (1488-1569) who was the first to publish a complete English Bible. Like Tyndale, Coverdale was forced to flee England for the Continent. He was thought to have assisted Tyndale in Hamburg and Antwerp. In 1533, King Henry VIII established the Church of England, and in 1534, the Upper House of Convocation of Canterbury petitioned King Henry to decree "that the holy scripture should be translated into the vulgar English tongue by certain good learned men, to be nominated by His Majesty, and should be delivered to the people for their instruction." Thomas Cromwell and Archbishop Cranmer were likewise convinced of the desirability of having the Bible translated into English. And so it appears that Tyndale's prayer was about to be answered.

Coverdale's Bible was printed in October 1535 and published under the title: "Biblia: The Bible, that is, the holy scripture of the Olde and New Testament, faithfully and truly translated out of Douche and Latyn in to Englishe MDXXXV." It was dedicated to King Henry VIII. The dedicatory epistle praises the king and denounces the errors of "the blind bishop of Rome." Two revised editions appeared in 1537. The first holds the distinction of being the earliest complete English Bible actually printed in England, while the second claimed the approbation: "Set forth with the King's most gracious license." A revised New Testament was issued in 1538 which contained the Latin in a parallel column.

Coverdale was more of an editor than a translator. He maintained that he "neither wrested nor altered so much as one word for the maintenance of any manner of sect: but have with a clear conscience purely and faithfully translated this out of five sundry interpreters, having only the manifest truth of the scripture before mine eyes." Some of these "five sundry interpreters" were mentioned on the title page: Douche

(German) and Latin. Coverdale based his work on the Zurich Bible of Zwingli, the Vulgate, the Latin text of Paginius, Luther's Bible, and the previous work of William Tyndale, especially in the New Testament. The Coverdale Bible was also the first to introduce chapter summaries instead of chapter headings. The order of books follows Tyndale and Luther: Hebrews, James, Jude, and Revelation are placed at the end of the New Testament, and the Apocrypha is segregated from the rest of the Old Testament.

The Matthew Bible

Although Coverdale's second edition of 1537 contained the license of the king, the first Bible to obtain such license was published earlier the same year. It was more of a revision than a translation, albeit the title was: "The Byble, which is all the holy Scripture: in whych are contayned the Olde and Newe Testament, truly and purely translated into Englysh by Thomas Matthew."

Thomas Matthew was just a pseudonym for John Rogers (c.1500-1555), a friend of Tyndale, to whom he had turned over his unpublished manuscripts on the translation of the Old Testament. Rogers used Tyndale's Pentateuch, Joshua to 2 Chronicles, and the 1535 revision of the New Testament. For the rest of the Bible, he relied on Coverdale. The whole of this material was slightly revised and accompanied by introductions and chapter summaries. The book order still followed the earlier Bibles of Tyndale and Coverdale. Cranmer commented in a letter to Cromwell that he liked it "better than any other translation heretofore made." And so it happened that Tyndale's translation, which was proscribed just a few years earlier, was circulating with the King's permission and authority both in the Coverdale and Matthew Bibles. Rogers was martyred in 1555 after the accession of Mary to the throne of England.

The Great Bible

Although the Coverdale and Matthew Bibles were "set forth with the King's most gracious license," the Great Bible was the first "authorized" Bible. Cromwell delegated to Myles Coverdale the work of revising the Matthew Bible along with its controversial notes. Printing was begun in Paris about May 1538. In September of the same year, an injunction by Cromwell directed the clergy to provide "one book of the bible of the largest volume in English, and the same set up in some convenient place within the said church that ye have care of, whereas your parishioners may most commodiously resort to the same and read it." Printing was delayed on account of the Inquisition, so the printing equipment was removed to London.

The completed Bible appeared in April of 1539, with the title page reading:

> The Byble in Englyshe, that is to saye the content of all the holy scrypture bothe of ye old and new testament, truly translated after the veryte of the Hebrue and Greke textes, by ye dylygent studye of dyverse excellent learned men, expert in the forsayde tonges. Prynted by Rychard Grafton and Edward Whitchurch. Cum privilegio ad imprimendum solum, 1539.

Although called the Great Bible because of its large size, it was referred to by several other designations as well. It was called the Cromwell Bible, since he did the most to prepare for its publication. It was also termed the Cranmer Bible after the often reprinted preface by Cranmer beginning with the 1540 second edition. Several editions were printed by Whitechurch, and hence it was labeled the Whitechurch Bible. In accordance with Cromwell's injunction, copies of the Great Bible were placed in every church and the Bible came to be called the Chained Bible, since it was chained in "some convenient place within the said church."

The Great Bible went through seven editions and was last printed in 1569. The second edition added the charge: "This is the Bible appointed to the use of the churches." It was still essentially the work of Tyndale: a revision of Matthew's Bible, which in turn was a revision of Tyndale's Bible. In the New Testament, the order of books follows the traditional arrangement seen in all ensuing versions.

The Taverner Bible

At the same time as Coverdale was preparing the Great Bible, Richard Taverner (1505-1577) undertook an independent revision of Matthew's Bible. It appeared under the title of: "The Most Sacred Bible whiche is the holy scripture, conteyning the old and new testament, translated into English, and newly recognized with great diligence after most faythful exemplars by Rychard Taverner." He was a competent Greek scholar and made some slight changes in the text and notes of the Matthew Bible. His work was eclipsed by the Great Bible and had but minor influence on later translations.

In the last years of the reign of Henry VIII, new laws restricting the circulation and reading of the Bible were made. In 1543, Parliament passed an act banning "the crafty, false and untrue translation of Tyndale." Notes in all other versions were to be expunged and it was made a crime for any unlicensed person to read the Bible. In 1546, the king himself ordained that "no man or woman" was to possess Tyndale's or Coverdale's New Testament. These Bibles were subsequently collected and burned.

Henry VIII died in January of 1547 and, at the accession of Edward VI, all prohibitions against the Bible were removed. During his reign, all the previous translations were frequently reprinted and churches were again directed to secure Bibles. But Edward's reign was short-lived. Mary Tudor came to the throne in 1553 and the Bible once again was restricted. John Rogers and Cranmer were executed while Myles Coverdale and other Reformers escaped to the Continent. Consequently, no Bibles were published in England during Mary's reign (1553-1558).

The Geneva Bible

During this time of exile on the Continent, many English Reformers, among them Myles Coverdale, settled in Geneva. It was here in 1557 that William Whittingham (1524-1579), the brother-in-law of Calvin, and successor of John Knox at the

English church in Geneva, translated the New Testament in what was to become the Geneva Bible. Whittingham had four English Bibles to work with as well as the newly published Greek editions of Stephanus and a new Latin translation by Beza. Three innovations were introduced in this New Testament which also appeared in the complete Geneva Bible. It was the first Bible to be printed in easy to read Roman type with italics denoting words added to complete the sense. The text was also divided into verses as found in the 1551 Greek New Testament of Stephanus.

Elizabeth assumed the throne in late 1558 and many exiles returned to England. But Whittingham, along with Anthony Gilby and Thomas Sampson, remained in Geneva and continued to work on a more comprehensive and complete revision of the entire Bible that superseded the 1557 New Testament. The Old Testament was likewise divided into verses as the New. This was done on the basis of the 1555 Latin Bible of Stephanus, the first Bible to show the present verse division in both Testaments. The new translation was issued in 1560, stating on the title page:

> The Bible and Holy Scriptures Conteyned in the Olde and Newe Testament. Translated according to the Ebrue and Greke, and conferred with the best translations in divers languages. With moste profitable annotations upon all the hard places, and other things of greate importance as may appeare in the Epistle to the Reader. "Feare not, stand stil, and beholde the salvacion of the Lord, which he wil shewe to you this day," Exod. xiv. 13. At Geneva. Printed by Rouland Hall, MDLX.

The Geneva Bible fast became immensely popular. Next to Tyndale, it had the most influence on the Authorized Version. It was dedicated to Queen Elizabeth and contained both Calvinistic and anti-Catholic notes. The Great Bible was still the Bible used in the churches, but the Geneva became the Bible of the people. It went through about 140 editions, the last one being in 1644. The New Testament was revised by Laurence Tomson in 1576 on the basis of Beza's Greek text with Latin version and commentary, published in 1565. In 1592, notes on Revelation by Franciscus Junis began to be added to make a third form of the Geneva Bible.

The Bishops Bible

The superiority of the Geneva Bible over the Great Bible was readily apparent, it was the notes, however, that made it unacceptable for official use in England. Archbishop Matthew Parker soon took steps to make a revision of the Great Bible that would replace both it and the Geneva Bible. The Bible was divided into parts and distributed to scholars for revision. Parker served as the editor and most of his revisors were bishops, hence the Bishops Bible. This was the first Bible to be translated by a committee. The work was finished in 1568 and a copy presented to the queen. The title was simply: "The holie Bible conteyning the olde Testament and the newe." Early editions contained the phrase "set forth by authority," while later ones read "authorized and appointed to be read in churches."

Because it was authorized by the bishops, the new Bible quickly displaced the Great Bible, which was not printed again after 1569. The instructions given to the revisors included:

> 1. Firste to followe the commune Englishe Translacion used in the Churches and not to recede from yt but wher yt varieth manifestlye from the Hebrue or Greke originall.
> 2. Item to make no bitter notis upon any text, or yet to set downe any determinacion in places of controversie.
> 3. Item that all such wordes as soundeth in the Olde Translacion to any offence of Lightnes or obscenitie be expressed with more convenient terms and phrases.

In 1571, the Convocation of Canterbury charged that "every archbishop and bishop should have at his house a copy of the holy Bible of the largest volume as lately printed at London." A revised version was issued in 1572 and a total of nineteen editions were produced, the last in 1602. The Geneva Bible was still the most popular, and began to be printed in England after the death of Archbishop Parker.

The Douay Rheims Bible

This was the first Roman Catholic translation of the Bible in English. It was Protestant exiles from England during the reign of Mary (1553-1558) who produced the Geneva Bible, but upon the accession of Elizabeth to the throne in November of 1558, the circumstances were reversed. It was now English Romanists who fled England for the Continent. Many settled in France, and in 1568 an English college was established by William Allen (1532-1594) at Douay. The college moved for a time to Rheims in 1578 under Richard Bristow (1538-1581). It was here that Gregory Martin (d.1582) began translating the Bible into English from the Latin Vulgate. This was precipitated by Allen's recognition that Catholics had an unfair disadvantage compared with Bible-reading Protestants:

Catholics educated in the academies and schools have hardly any knowledge of the Scriptures except in Latin. When they are preaching to the unlearned and are obliged on the spur of the moment to translate some passage into the vernacular they often do it inaccurately and with unpleasant hesitation because either there is no vernacular version of the words, or it does not occur to them at the moment. Our adversaries however, have at their finger tips from some heretical version all those passages of scripture which seem to make for them, and by a certain deceptive adaptation and alteration of the sacred words produce the effect of appearing to say nothing but what comes from the Bible. This evil might be remedied if we too had some Catholic version of the Bible, for all the English versions are most corrupt.

The Bible was finished in 1582, but only the New Testament was published at that time:

THE NEW TESTAMENT OF JESUS CHRIST

TRANSLATED FAITHFULLY INTO ENGLISH, OUT OF THE AUTHENTICAL LATIN, according to the best corrected copies of the same; diligently conferred with the Greeke and other Editions in divers languages; with Arguments of Bookes and Chapters, Annotations, and other necessarie helps for the better understanding of the text, and specially for the discoverie of the Corruptions of divers late translations, and for cleering the Controversies in Religion of these daies; In the *English College of Rhemes*. Printed at Rhemes by John Fogney 1582 cum privilegio.

In this same year, Gregory Martin wrote a book with the imposing title of:

A DISCOVERIE of the Manifold Corruptions of the Holie Scriptures by the Heretikes of our daies, specially the English Sectaries, and of their foule dealing herein, by partial and false translations, to the advantage of their heresies, in their English Bibles used and authorised since the time of the Schisme, by Gregorie Martin, one of the Readers of Divinitie in the English College of Rhemes.

The college returned to Douay in 1593, and the Old Testament, translated, but yet unprinted for lack of funds, was published in two volumes in 1609-10, the complete title page reading:

THE HOLY BIBLE FAITHFULLY TRANSLATED INTO ENGLISH, out of the Authentical Latin; diligently conferred with the Hebrew, Greeke, and other Editions in divers languages; with Arguments of the Bookes, and Chapters, Annotations, Tables, and other helps for better understanding of the text, for the discoverie of Corruptions in some late translations, and for the clearing Controversies in Religion; by THE ENGLISH COLLEGE OF DOUAY, *Printed at Douay,* by *Lawrence Kellam,* at the signe of the Holie Lambe, 1609.

Since the Old Testament was published at Douay and the New at Rheims, it was only natural that this Roman Catholic translation be referred to as the Douay Rheims Bible. Like the Geneva Bible, this version had numerous notes to establish the doctrines of the translators. This was previously recognized by William Allen: "There is often such need of reading the scriptures in order to confute our opponents, it is better that there should be a faithful and catholic translation than that men should use a corrupt version to their peril or destruction; the more so since the dangers which arise from reading certain more difficult passages my be alleviated by suitable notes."

The New Testament of the Douay Rheims Bible underwent three more editions: 1600, 1621, and 1633, while the Old Testament went through another in 1635. It was not until 100 years later that any more revisions were done. In 1749, Bishop Richard Challoner (1691-1781) brought out his revision of the Rheims New Testament:

> The New Testament of our Lord and Saviour Jesus Christ. Translated out of the Latin Vulgat: diligently compared with the original Greek; and first published by the English College at Rhemes, Anno 1582. Newly revised and corrected according to the Clementin edition of the Scriptures. With Annotations for clearing up modern Controversies in Religion, and other Difficulties of Holy Writ. Printed in the year MDCCX-LIX.

A revision of the Old Testament followed in 1750 along with additional changes to the New. The whole was revised again in 1763-64 and 1772. All further editions of the Douay Rheims Bible were dependent on one or another of Challoner's revisions. Bernard MacMahon (c.1736-1816) made a further series of revisions during the period from 1783-1810. Many other editions followed through the years by Coyne, Haydock, and others. In 1829, the Provincial Council of Baltimore sought to produce as correct edition as possible. This was accomplished through the efforts of Francis Kenrick (1797-1863), bishop of

Philadelphia, who brought out a revision of the Gospels in 1849, and the completed Bible in 1860. Other minor revisions continued to appear until the publication of the Confraternity Version in 1941.

The King James Bible

As the reign of Elizabeth (1558-1603) was coming to a close, we find a draft for an act of Parliament for a new version of the Bible: "An act for the reducing of diversities of bibles now extant in the English tongue to one settled vulgar translated from the original." The Bishop's Bible of 1568, although it may have eclipsed the Great Bible, was still rivaled by the Geneva Bible. Nothing ever became of this draft during the reign of Elizabeth, who died in 1603, and was succeeded by James I, as the throne passed from the Tudors to the Stuarts. James was at that time James VI of Scotland, and had been for thirty-seven years. He was born during the period between the Geneva and the Bishop's Bible.

One of the first things done by the new king was the calling of the Hampton Court Conference in January of 1604 "for the hearing, and for the determining, things pretended to be amiss in the church." Here were assembled bishops, clergyman, and professors, along with four Puritan divines, to consider the complaints of the Puritans. Although Bible revision was not on the agenda, the Puritan president of Corpus Christi College, John Reynolds, "moved his Majesty, that there might be a new translation of the Bible, because those which were allowed in the reigns of Henry the eighth, and Edward the sixth, were corrupt and not answerable to the truth of the Original."

The king rejoined that he:

> Could never yet see a Bible well translated in English; but I think that, of all, that of Geneva is the worst. I wish some special pains were taken for an uniform translation, which should be done by the best learned men in both Universities, then reviewed by the Bishops, presented to the Privy Council, lastly ratified by Royal authority, to be read in the whole Church,

and none other.

Accordingly, a resolution came forth:

> That a translation be made of the whole Bible, as
> consonant as can be to the original Hebrew and Greek;
> and this to be set out and printed, without any
> marginal notes, and only to be used in all churches of
> England in time of divine service.

The next step was the actual selection of the men who were
to perform the work. In July of 1604, James wrote to Bishop
Bancroft that he had "appointed certain learned men, to the
number of four and fifty, for the translating of the Bible." These
men were the best biblical scholars and linguists of their day. In
the preface to their completed work it is further stated that
"there were many chosen, that were greater in other men's eyes
than in their own, and that sought the truth rather than their own
praise. Again, they came or were thought to come to the work,
learned, not to learn." Other men were sought out, according to
James, "so that our said intended translation may have the help
and furtherance of all our principal learned men within this our
kingdom."

Although fifty-four men were nominated, only forty-seven
were known to have taken part in the work of translation. The
translators were organized into six groups, and met respectively
at Westminster, Cambridge, and Oxford. Ten at Westminster
were assigned Genesis through 2 Kings; seven had Romans
through Jude. At Cambridge, eight worked on 1 Chronicles
through Ecclesiastes, while seven others handled the Apocrypha.
Oxford employed seven to translate Isaiah through Malachi;
eight occupied themselves with the Gospels, Acts, and Revelation.

Fifteen general rules were advanced for the guidance of the
translators:

> 1. The ordinary Bible read in the Church, commonly
> called the *Bishops Bible,* to be followed, and as little
> altered as the Truth of the original will permit.

2. The names of the Prophets, and the Holy Writers, with the other Names of the Text, to be retained, as nigh as may be, accordingly as they were vulgarly used.

3. The Old Ecclesiastical Words to be kept, *viz.* the Word *Church* not to be translated *Congregation* &c.

4. When a Word hath divers Significations, that to be kept which hath been most commonly used by the most of the Ancient Fathers, being agreeable to the Propriety of the Place, and the Analogy of the Faith.

5. The Division of the Chapters to be altered, either not at all, or as little as may be, if Necessity so require.

6. No Marginal Notes at all to be affixed, but only for the explanation of the *Hebrew* or *Greek* Words, which cannot without some circumlocution, so briefly and fitly be expressed in the Text.

7. Such Quotations of Places to be marginally set down as shall serve for the fit Reference of one Scripture to another.

8. Every particular Man of each Company, to take the same Chapter or Chapters, and having translated or amended them severally by himself, where he thinketh good, all to meet together, confer what they have done, and agree for their Parts what shall stand.

9. As any one Company hath dispatched any one Book in this Manner they shall send it to the rest, to be consider'd of seriously and judiciously, for His Majesty is very careful in this Point.

10. If any Company, upon the Review of the Book so sent, doubt or differ upon any Place, to send them Word thereof; note the Place, and withal send the Reasons, to which if they consent not, the Difference to be compounded at the general Meeting, which is to be of the chief Persons of each Company, at the end of the Work.

11. When any Place of special Obscurity is doubted of, Letters to be directed by Authority, to send to any Learned Man in the Land, for his Judgement of such a Place.

12. Letters to be sent from every Bishop to the rest of his Clergy, admonishing them of this Translation in hand; and to move and charge as many skilful in the

Tongues; and having taken pains in that kind, to send his particular Observations to the Company, either at *Westminster, Cambridge, or Oxford.*

13. The Directors in each Company, to be the Deans of *Westminster,* and *Chester* for that Place; and the King's Professors in the *Hebrew* or *Greek* in either University.

14. These translations to be used when they agree better with the Text than the Bishops Bible: Tindoll's, Matthews, Coverdale's, Whitchurch's, Geneva.

15. Besides the said Directors before mentioned, three or four of the most Ancient and Grave Divines, in either of the Universities, not employed in Translating, to be assigned by the vice-Chancellor, upon Conference with the rest of the Heads, to be Overseers of the Translations as well *Hebrew* as *Greek,* for the better observation of the 4th Rule above specified.

The work began to take shape in 1604 and progressed steadily. The translators expressed their early thoughts in their preface as: "Truly (good Christian Reader) we never thought from the beginning, that we should need to make a new Translation, nor yet to make of a bad one a good one,... but to make a good one better, or out of many good ones, one principal good one, not justly to be excepted against, that hath been our endeavor."

They had at their disposal all the previous English translations to which they did not disdain:

We are so far off from condemning any of their labors that travailed before us in this kind, either in this land or beyond sea, either in King Henry's time, or King Edward's ... or Queen Elizabeth's of everrenowned memory, that we acknowledge them to have been raised up of God, for the building and furnishing of his Church, and that they deserve to be had of us and of posterity in everlasting remembrance.

And, as the translators themselves also acknowledged, they had a multitude of sources from which to draw from: "Neither did we think much to consult the Translators or Commentators,

Chaldee, Hebrew, Syrian, Greek, or Latin, no nor the Spanish, French, Italian, or Dutch." The Greek editions of Erasmus, Stephanus, and Beza were all accessible, as were the Complutensian and Antwerp Polyglots, and the Latin translations of Pagninus, Tremellius, and Beza.

Four years were spent on the preliminary translation by the six groups. The translators were exacting and particular in their work, as related in their preface:

> Neither did we disdain to revise that which we had done, and to bring back to the anvil that which we had hammered: but having and using as great helps as were needful, and fearing no reproach for slowness, nor coveting praise for expedition, we have at the length, through the good hand of the Lord upon us, brought the work to that pass that you see.

The conferences of each of the six being ended, nine months were spent at Stationers' Hall in London for review and revision of the work by two men each from the Westminster, Cambridge, and Oxford companies. The final revision was then completed by Myles Smith and Thomas Bilson, with a preface supplied by Smith.

The completed work was issued in 1611:

> THE HOLY BIBLE, Conteyning the Old Testament, AND THE NEW: Newly Translated out of the Originall tongues: & with the former Translations diligently compared and revised, by his Majesties Special Commandment. Appointed to be read in Churches. Imprinted at London by Robert Barker, Printer to the Kings most Excellent Majestie. ANNO DOM. 1611.

The New Testament had a separate title page reading:

> THE NEWE Testament of our Lord and Saviour JESUS CHRIST. Newly Translated out of the Originall Greeke: and with the former Translations diligently compared and revised, by his Majesties speciall

Commandment. IMPRINTED at London by Robert Barker, Printer to the Kings most Excellent Majestie. ANNO DOM. 1611. *Cum Privilegio.*

The King James Bible was, in its first editions, even larger than the Great Bible. It was printed in black letter with small italicized Roman type to represent those words not in the original languages.

A dedicatory epistle to King James, which also enhanced the completed work, recalled the King's desire that "there should be one more exact Translation of the holy Scriptures into the *English tongue.*" The translators expressed that they were "poor Instruments to make GODS holy Truth to be yet more and more known," while at the same time recognizing that "Popish persons" sought to keep the people "in ignorance and darkness."

The Authorized Version, as it came to be called, went through several editions and revisions. Two notable editions were that of 1629, the first ever printed at Cambridge, and that of 1638, also at Cambridge, which was assisted by John Bois and Samuel Ward, two of the original translators. In 1657, the Parliament considered another revision, but it came to naught. The most important editions were those of the 1762 Cambridge revision by Thomas Paris, and the 1769 Oxford revision by Benjamin Blayney. One of the earliest concordances was *A Concordance to the Bible of the Last Translation,* by John Downham, affixed to a printing of 1632. The Authorized Version eclipsed all previous versions of the Bible. The Geneva Bible was last printed in 1644, but the notes continued to be published with the King James text. Subsequent versions of the Bible were likewise eclipsed, for the Authorized Version was *the Bible* until the advent of the Revised Version and ensuing modern translations. It is still accepted as such by its defenders, and recognized as so by its detractors.

Alexander Geddes (d.1802), a Roman Catholic priest, who in 1792 issued the first volume of his own translation of the Bible, accordingly paid tribute to *the Bible* of his time:

The highest eulogiums have been made on the

translation of James the First, both by our own writers and by foreigners. And, indeed, if accuracy, fidelity, and the strictest attention to the letter of the text, be supposed to constitute the qualities of an excellent version, this of all versions, must, in general, be accounted the most excellent. Every sentence, every work, every syllable, every letter and point, seem to have been weighed with the nicest exactitude; and expressed, either in the text, or margin, with the greatest precision.

As to whether the Authorized Version was ever officially "authorized," Brooke Westcott, one of the members of the committee that produced the Revised Version, and the editor, with Fenton Hort, of an edition of the Greek New Testament, stated that:

From the middle of the seventeenth century, the King's Bible has been the acknowledged Bible of the English-speaking nations throughout the world simply because it is the best. A revision which embodied the ripe fruits of nearly a century of labour, and appealed to the religious instinct of a great Christian people, gained by its own internal character a vital authority which could never have been secured by any edict of sovereign rulers.

There is no parallel in literary or religious history to the period from Tyndale to the Authorized Version of 1611.

CHAPTER THREE

THE SOUND OF SILENCE

Although there were an abundance of further attempts at translating the Bible into English after the appearance of the Authorized Version, there is scarcely any public knowledge of such efforts due to the overwhelming approbation and acceptance of that translation. It was not until the arrival of the Revised Version in 1881-85 that anything seriously challenged the ascendancy of the Authorized Version. The principal thing about this otherwise tacit period was the development of the science of textual criticism, as respecting the Greek New Testament. Accordingly, a compact survey of the development of the Greek New Testament in its critical editions is essential to lay the groundwork for an examination of English Bible translations in this period.

The Greek New Testament

The establishment of the Received Text characterized the early period of English Bible translations from Tyndale to King James. The era from that time up to the age of the critical text beginning with Westcott and Hort is marked, first of all, by the collection of evidence, and secondly, by the utilization of such evidence to produce a critical text that differed perceivably from the Received Text.

The first systematic assembly of variant readings was that of the six volume London Polyglot issued by Brian Walton (1600-1661) in 1655-57. Walton's Polyglot was the first to make use of Codex Alexandrinus as well as sixteen other recently collated manuscripts. In 1675, John Fell (1625-1686) issued an edition of the Greek New Testament, the first to be published at

Oxford. He gave variants from over 100 manuscripts supplemented by Coptic and Gothic versions. The foundations of textual criticism can be traced to Richard Simon (1638-1712), a French Roman Catholic. His four notable publications (1689-1695), which critically examined the text of the Bible as a piece of literature, anticipated later conclusions of other editors. John Mill (1645-1707) issued an edition of the Greek New Testament in 1707 citing over 30,000 variants. He added evidence from seventy-eight new manuscripts and made extensive use of patristic quotations.

Edward Wells (1667-1727) was the first to actually depart from the Received Text in his edition of the Greek New Testament published between 1709 and 1719. Richard Bentley (1662-1742) announced proposals in 1720 for his Greek New Testament which would restore the ancient text. Although his work was never published, he had an influence on subsequent editors. The next Greek edition to appear was that of Daniel Mace (d.1753). It was issued in 1729 with an English translation and corrected the Received Text with variant readings from Mill's apparatus. In 1734, John Bengel (1687-1752) published his edition of the Greek New Testament in which he sought to classify and weigh manuscripts. John Wettstein (1693-1754), who collated manuscripts for Bentley, issued his edition in 1751-52. He printed the Elzevir text with his corrections in the margin.

Over in England, William Bowyer (1699-1777) produced a critical edition of the Greek New Testament in 1763. He introduced square brackets to mark readings which he deemed did not have the support of good manuscripts. John Semler (1725-1791) issued no Greek Testament of his own, but perfected the "family classification" system of Bengel. This in turn was duplicated by John Griesbach (1745-1812), who published a three-volume edition of the Greek New Testament in 1775-77. A second edition followed in 1796-1806. Christian Matthaei (1744-1811) published his first edition of the Greek New Testament in 1782-88. A second edition appeared in 1803-07. The chief importance of his work was his accurate citation of many manuscripts. Two Roman Catholic scholars followed suit. Franz Alter (1749-1804) published an edition of the Greek New Testament in 1786-87. It was based on one manuscript, but cited evidence from twenty others plus the Bohairic version and four Slavic manuscripts. John Scholz (1794-1852), published an edition in 1830-36 which cited more than 600 manuscripts.

The second milestone during the period of the development of the critical text was the work of Karl Lachmann (1793-1851), the first recognized scholar to completely disregard the Received Text. He issued his first edition of the Greek New Testament in 1831 and the second in 1842-50. Relying strictly on ancient witnesses, Lachmann sought to restore the fourth century text. Constantine Tischendorf (1815-1874) located and published more manuscripts and edited more editions of the Greek New Testament than anyone else. He published seven editions from 1841 to 1859. He was also the discover of Codex Sinaiticus, which culminated in his eighth (1859-72), and most important, edition of the Greek New Testament, based largely on that codex.

Throughout the many years of Tischendorf's work, others continued to bring forth more critical editions of the Greek Testament. Henry Alford (1810-1871) published six editions of his Greek New Testament between 1849 and 1861. Samuel Tregelles (1813-1875) produced but one edition of the Greek New Testament. It was published at London in six parts between 1857 and 1872. During the later half of the nineteenth century, F.H.A. Scrivener (1813-1891) reissued the Textus Receptus in several editions.

Although none of the English Bible translations produced during the period between the Authorized and Revised Versions had any effect on the circulation of the Authorized Version, there are many significant versions to observe in order to make this history complete. This interval, between what for a short time were two rival versions, is to be noted for the worldwide distribution of the word of God and the formation of various Bible Societies for this purpose. The British and Foreign Bible Society was formed in 1804. This was followed in America by the Philadelphia Bible Society in 1808 and the American Bible Society in 1816. Back in London in 1831, the Trinitarian Bible Society was started over a controversy with the British and

Foreign Bible Society. The American and Foreign Bible Society was begun by Baptists in 1836 who left the American Bible Society. The Baptists also formed the American Bible Union in 1850. During the Civil War, the Confederate States Bible Society was organized in 1862.

The first English Bible printed in America was an Authorized Version by Robert Aitken. The New Testament was published in 1777:

> The New Testament of our Lord and Saviour Jesus Christ; Newly Translated out of the Original Greek; And with the former Translations Diligently compared and revised. Appointed to be read in Churches. Philadelphia: Printed and Sold by R. Aitken, Printer and Bookseller, Front Street. 1777. *Spectamur agendo.*

Other editions were published in 1778, 1779, and 1781. The complete Bible was published in 1782:

> The Holy Bible, Containing the Old and New Testaments: Newly translated out of the Original Tongues; And with the former Translations Diligently compared and revised. Philadelphia: Printed and Sold by R. Aitken, at Pope's Head, Three Doors above the Coffee House, in Market Street. MDCCLXXXII.

This edition of the Authorized Version of the Bible was actually recommended by the United States government to its citizens:

> *Resolved,* That the United States in Congress assembled, highly approve the pious and laudable undertaking of Mr. Aitken, as subservient to the interest of religion as well as the progress of the arts in this country, and being satisfied from the above report, of his care and accuracy in the execution of the work, they recommend this edition of the Bible to the inhabitants of the United States, and hereby authorize him to publish this recommendation in the manner he shall think proper.

In addition to these enumerated translations, there are also a multitude of partial and unfinished attempts. Early versions in this period were mainly revisions of the Authorized Version, but after the publication of the critical Greek texts, many completely new translations were undertaken from them. It should also be noted that a shift takes place beginning in the later part of the nineteenth century from England to America. The principal versions in this period will be surveyed with the rest appearing in the Appendix.

1653

A Paraphrase, and Annotations Upon all the Books of the New Testament

This was one of the first attempts since the Authorized Version to produce a new translation. It was the work of Henry Hammond (1605-1660), who assisted Brian Walton in the preparation of the London Polyglot. Several editions of this paraphrase, which prints the Authorized Version in a parallel column, were subsequently published, the last edition being in four volumes in 1845.

1657

The Dutch Annotations upon the whole Bible

The Synod of Dort in 1618 ordered a new translation of the Bible into Dutch. This version was published in 1637 and translated, by request of Parliament, into English in 1657. The translator was Theodore Haak, who was often employed by the English government to translate foreign documents.

1685

New Testament with a paraphrase and notes

This is the work of Richard Baxter, a Nonconformist minister in England. A second edition was issued in 1695.

1703

Paraphrase and Commentary on the New Testament

This popular work by Daniel Whitby (1638-1726) also appeared in a second edition in 1706, a third in 1709-10, and a fourth in 1759-60. Whitby was a chaplain to the bishop of Salisbury and was widely known for the publication of his anti-Catholic writings between 1664 and 1688. He is foremost remembered for his development of Postmillennialism.

1718

The New Testament

This was the first new Roman Catholic translation to appear since the Douay Rheims. A corrected edition was issued in 1719. The translator was Cornelius Nary (1660-1737), a parish priest in Dublin. Speaking of both the Old and New Testaments of the Douay Rheims Bible, Nary maintained that "the Language whereof is so old, the Words in many places so obsolete, the Orthography so bad, and the Translation so very literal, that in a number of Places it is unintelligible, and all over so grating to the Ears of such as are accustomed to speak, in a manner, another Language, that most People will not be at the Pains of reading them." His new translation was from the Latin Vulgate and the complete title was:

The New Testament of our Lord and Saviour Jesus Christ. Newly translated out of the Latin Vulgat, and with the Original Greek, and divers Translations in Vulgar Languages diligently compared and revised. Together with Annotations upon the most remarkable Passages in the Gospels, and Marginal Notes upon other difficult Texts of the same, and upon the rest of the books of the new Testament, for the better understanding of the literal Sense.

Nary claimed of his work that he "endeavored to make this New

Testament speak the English tongue now used." He also maintained that he took "all the care imaginable to keep as close to the letter as the English will permit."

1724

The Common Translation corrected, with a paraphrase and notes

The New Testament of this work, translated by Edward Wells (1667-1727), first appeared in 1718. He aimed to revise the Authorized Version. This was probably the first attempt to revise the Old Testament along with the New.

1729

The New Testament in Greek and English

After first constructing a critical edition of the Greek New Testament, Daniel Mace (d.1753), a Presbyterian minister, issued his new English translation based on it. Both texts were printed in diglot form and entitled:

> The New Testament in Greek and English. Containing the Original Text Corrected from the Authority of the Most Authentic Manuscripts: and a New Version form'd agreeably to the Illustrations of the most Learned Commentators and Critics: with Notes and Various Readings, and a Copious Alphabetical Index.

Verse numbers are in the margins and sentences begin with a capital letter only at the beginning of a new paragraph. The translation is in a terse colloquial style.

1730

Annotations on the New Testament of Jesus Christ

Translated by Robert Witham (d.1738), president of the

college at Douay when Richard Challoner served as vice-president, this Roman Catholic translation was in two volumes and contained numerous notes. It was translated from the Latin Vulgate and the complete original title read:

> Annotations on the New Testament of Jesus Christ, in which:
> I. The Literal sense is explained according to the Expositions of the Ancient Fathers.
> II. The false Interpretations, both of the ancient and modern writers, which are contrary to the received Doctrine of the Catholic Church, are briefly examined and disproved.
> III. With an account of the chief differences betwixt the text of the ancient Latin Version and the Greek in the printed Editions and MSS. By R.W. DD.

Challoner himself claimed to have examined "the English translation of the whole New Testament and have found it faithful in every respect and in conformity with the Vulgate." In support of his translation, Whitham pointed out that the Douay Rheims Bible was made before the corrections to the Vulgate were done under Pope Sixtus V in 1592 and Pope Clement VIII in 1598. A second edition appeared in 1733 and a third in 1740.

The New Testament

This is a translation into English by William Webster (1689-1758) of the French version of Richard Simon (1638-1712).

1745

Primitive New Testament

William Whiston (1667-1752), the translator of this work, is best remembered for his translation of Josephus still widely used today. He published his edition of the New Testament when he was seventy-eight years old. He basically follows the Authorized Version except when it departs from what he considered to be the "primitive" text.

1752

Exposition of the New Testament in the form of a Paraphrase

Issued in three volumes beginning in 1739, this translation was the work of John Guyse, an Independent minister who was a vigorous opponent of Arianism. It went through several editions, the sixth of which being published in 1818.

1755

Explanatory Notes on the New Testament

This is the translation by John Wesley (1703-1791), the founder of Methodism. It was based on the Authorized Version, revised and altered as he saw fit. Wesley asserted that he "never knowingly so much as in one place altered it for altering's sake: But there, and there only, where, First, The Sense was made better, stronger, clearer, or more consistent with the Context: Secondly, Where, the Sense being equally good, the Phrase was better or nearer the Original." It went through several more editions including 1760, 1768, 1790, and 1839.

1756

Family Expositor, or, a Paraphrase and Version of the New Testament

This is the translation by Philip Doddridge (1702-1751) that was later used by the Presbyterians in 1818. It was issued in six volumes beginning in 1739. An American edition was published in 1808.

1761

An Interpretation of the New Testament

The Gospels of this New Testament by John Heylin

(c.1685-1759) were first published in 1749 and the completed work after his death.

1764

A new and literal translation of all the books of the Old and New Testament

This is the Quaker Bible of Anthony Purver (1702-1777) that took him thirty years to translate.

The New Testament: carefully collated with the Greek, and corrected

This translation is the work of Richard Wynne in which he sought "to steer in a just medium between a servile literal translation, and a paraphrastic loose version; between low, obsolete, and obscure language, and a modern enervated style." The text is printed in paragraphs instead of verses.

1765

A New Translation of the New Testament

Translated by Samuel Palmer, this version was based on the earlier paraphrase of Philip Doddridge but with some revision.

1768

A Liberal Translation of the New Testament

This translation by Edward Harwood (1729-1794) was said by him to be "not a verbal translation, but a *liberal* and *diffusive* version of the sacred classics, and is calculated to answer the purpose of an explanatory paraphrase as well as a free and elegant translation." The complete title page read:

A Liberal Translation of the New Testament; being an Attempt to translate the Sacred Writings with the same

Freedom, Spirit, and Elegance, with which other English Translations from the Greek Classics have lately been executed: The Design and Scope of each Author being strictly and impartially explored, the True Significance and Force of the Original critically observed, and, as much as possible, transfused into our Language, and the Whole elucidated and explained upon a new and rational Plan: With Select Notes, Critical and Explanatory. By E. Harwood. London, MDCCLXVIII.

Harwood's purpose in making this translation was stated as:

Such a Translation of the New Testament might induce persons of a liberal education and polite state to peruse the sacred volume, and that such a version might prove of signal service to the cause of truth, liberty and Christianity if men of cultivated and improved minds, especially YOUTH, could be allured by the innocent stratagem of a *modern style,* to read a book, which is now, alas! too generally neglected and disregarded by the young and gay, as a volume containing little to amuse and delight.

Harwood also made translations from the French and German and was learned in the textual criticism of the New Testament.

1770

The New Testament or New Covenant of our Lord and Saviour Jesus Christ

This translation by John Worsley (d.1767), which was edited by his son and published after his death, is said to be "translated from the Greek according to the Present Idiom." It was one of the first modern speech versions. Worsley advocated the retranslation of the Bible into the current speech at least once a century. He claims that he tried not only "to make the form of expression more suitable to our present language," but to bring it "nearer to the original."

1791

A Translation of the New Testament

The translator, Gilbert Wakefield (1756-1801), a Unitarian, had already published *A new translation of those parts only of the New Testament which are wrongly translated in our common version.* Consequently, his translation follows the Authorized Version to a great degree. Wakefield stated his chief rule as "to adopt the received version upon all possible occasions, and never to supersede it unless some low, obsolete or obscure word, some vulgar idiom, some coarse or uncouth phrase" require an alteration in the text. A second edition was issued in 1795.

1795

A Translation of the New Testament from the original Greek

This work was translated by Thomas Haweis (1734-1820), a Methodist minister and one of the founders of the London Missionary Society. He claimed that his translation was "humbly attempted with a view to assist the unlearned with clearer and more explicit views of the mind of the Spirit in the Scriptures of Truth."

1796

The New Testament

Although printed in 1796, evidently this translation was not published until after the author's death. In 1792, the translator, William Newcome (1729-1800) published *An Historical View of the English Biblical Translations* in which he advocated that the Authorized Version be revised. A revision of some Old Testament books was undertaken before Newcome's New Testament was published as:

An Attempt towards revising our English Translation

of the Greek Scriptures, or the New Covenant of Jesus Christ: and towards illustrating the sense by philological and explanatory notes.

The work was based in part on Griesbach's Greek New Testament published in 1775-77.

1798

A Translation of the New Testament from the Original Greek

This is the work of Nathaniel Scarlett (1753-1802), who at first was a Methodist, then a Universalist, and finally a Baptist. The work maintains to be "humbly attempted by Nathaniel Scarlett, assisted by men of piety & literature." It was based on a manuscript translation by James Creighton, who met once a week with Scarlett and others to revise his translation. The final readings are Scarlett's however. He further stated in his Preface: "Whilst an attempt is made to bring this sacred Book somewhat nearer to the English idiom at this day, still care is taken to steer between the two extremes, of being too servile and literal one the one hand, or too periphrastic on the other."

1799

A Revised Translation and Interpretation of the Sacred Scriptures

The work of J.M. Ray (1750-1816), this translation asserts to be "after the Eastern manner, from concurrent authorities of the critics, interpreters, and commentators, copies and versions: showing that the inspired writings contain the seeds of valuable sciences."

1808

The Holy Bible containing The Old and New Covenant

This was the first complete translation of the Bible into

English by an American. It was also the first English translation from the Septuagint. The translator, Charles Thomson (1729-1824), was at one time the secretary of the Continental Congress. His translation was also referred to by the American Revision Committee of the Revised Version.

The New Testament, in an improved version

This was a Unitarian translation by Thomas Belsham (1750-1829), who also published under his own name a translation of the Pauline Epistles. It was based on the New Testament by William Newcome. It was not until the fifth edition of 1819 that the title was actually called the Unitarian Version.

1823

The New Testament

Originally published in the same year as part of a Greek-English diglot, this translation by Abner Kneeland (1774-1844) was prepared "upon the basis of the fourth London edition of the Improved version, with an attempt to further improvement from the translations of Campbell, Wakefield, Scarlett, MacKnight and Thomson." Kneeland was originally a Baptist, but later became a Universalist and then a Deist.

1826

The Sacred Writings of the Apostles and Evangelists of Jesus Christ

This New Testament translation was by Alexander Campbell (1788-1866), primary founder of the Disciples of Christ (Church of Christ or Campbellites). Campbell at first desired to publish the Presbyterian edition of the New Testament that had appeared in London in 1818. Failing that attempt, he undertook a revision of it based on the critical Greek Testament of Griesbach. This 1818 New Testament contained the work of three men who originally issued separate translations. In 1795, James Macknight published *A New Literal Translation from the Original Greek, of the Apostolical Epistles.* Not being satisfied with any translation up to his time, James Macknight believed that "a translation of the sacred writings, more agreeable to the original, and more intelligible and unambiguous than any hitherto extant, is much wanted." Concluding that all former translations erred by "copying those who went before them," this translation was supposedly made from "the original itself." In 1789, George Campbell translated the Gospels "with preliminary dissertations, and notes critical and explanatory." It went through several editions and was published prior to the 1818 New Testament with Macknight's Epistles. The Acts and Book of Revelation were taken from the aforementioned Doddridge version of 1756, which was first printed in American in 1808. Campbell's translation went through several later editions.

1833

The Webster Bible

This is a revision of the Authorized Version by Noah Webster (1758-1843), compiler of Webster's Dictionary. The complete title was: "The Holy Bible, containing the Old and New Testaments, in the Common Version; with Amendments of the language, by Noah Webster, LL.D." Regarding the Authorized Version, Webster believed that "the general style of the version ought not to be altered" and that its language "is in general correct and perspicuous." His desire was to correct "inaccuracies in grammar," "quaint and vulgar phrases," and "a few errors in the translation." Webster held that alterations in the popular version of the Scriptures should be infrequent and that any Bible amended such "may require no alteration for two or three centuries to come." A second edition was published in 1841 and the New Testament was issued separately in 1839.

A New and Corrected Version of the New Testament

Translated by Rodolphus Dickinson (1787-1863), an Episcopalian rector, this is another version based on the Greek text of

Griesbach. Dickinson condemns the "quaint monotony and affected solemnity" of the Authorized Version and accuses it of "frequently rude and occasionally barbarous attire." He claims that he made his translation because he felt that "the errors in grammar and rhetoric, the harsh and indelicate expressions, dispersed through the generally adopted text, demand amendment." He sought to adorn the Scriptures with "a splendid and sweetly flowing diction" suited to the use of "accomplished and refined persons."

1840

The New Testament

This version by Edgar Taylor (1793-1839), was published just after his death. It was a revision of the Authorized Version "with the aid of other translations and made conformable to the Greek text of J.J. Griesbach."

1841

The Holy Bible

This is the work of John Conquest (1789-1844) that contained the text of the Authorized Version but "with twenty thousand emendations."

1850

The New Testament

Although based on the Authorized Version, this version contained "several hundred emendations." The editors, Spencer Cone (1785-1855) and William Wyckoff (1807-1876), were both Baptists who were influential in the founding of the American and Foreign Bible Society in 1836 and the American Bible Union in 1850. The editors claim that they "have removed many of the most objectionable blemishes and so far made a good translation better."

1858

The New Testament, Translated from the Original Greek

This translation is the sole work of Leicester Sawyer (1807-1898), who stated: "It is an unfortunate result of King James's translation of the Bible by an imposing council of learned men, that it has tended to discourage individual effort in respect to a labor of this kind, and to create a prejudice against it as necessarily incompetent and untrustworthy." This version has the order of books and the divisions of chapters and verses altered. A second edition was revised to conform to Tischendorf's Greek text, and a new edition was issued in 1891.

1863

The Holy Bible

This is the work of Robert Young (1822-1888), best known for his Analytical Concordance to the Bible that went through several editions. It came to be known as Young's Literal Translation of the Bible. Young deemed this translation "not to be considered as intended to come into competition with the *ordinary* use of the commonly received English Version of the Holy Scriptures, but simply as a strictly literal and idiomatic rendering of the Original Hebrew and Greek Texts." The Greek text followed is acknowledged to be the Received Text. Special attention was paid in this work to the proper translation of the Hebrew verb.

1864

American Bible Union Version

The American Bible Union was formed in 1850 by Baptists who wanted to produce an "immersionist" version. The rules governing those employed to revise the common Bible were:

1. The received Greek text, critically edited, with known errors corrected, must be followed.

2. The common English version must be the basis of revision, and only such alterations must be made as the exact meaning of the text and the existing state of the language may require.

3. The exact meaning of the inspired text, as that text expressed it to those who understood the original Scriptures at the time they were first written, must be given in corresponding words and phrases, so far as they can be found in the English language, with the least possible obscurity or indefiniteness.

Each book was produced by a single translator, the first of which was completed in 1852, and the entire New Testament in 1864. Thomas Conant was one of the main editors and translators. It went through several editions and was finally revised and published with the completed Old Testament in 1912.

1865

The Holy Bible

This marks the completion of the Bible translation by the Unitarian Samuel Sharpe (1799-1881). The New Testament was published in 1840 "translated from the Greek of J.J. Griesbach." His Old Testament was a revision of the Authorized Version. Sharpe revised both his Testaments several times, with the last edition of the Old Testament being in 1881.

1867

The Holy Scriptures

This is the translation by the Mormon prophet and founder Joseph Smith (1805-1844). It is accepted today by the Reorganized Church of Jesus Christ of Latter Day Saints. It is supposed to be an "inspired revision" of the Authorized Version, and it is today entitled the Inspired Version. Smith based his revision on a "direct revelation" which he claimed to have received in 1830. Many books and chapters that were deemed "correct" were left as is, but many "plain and precious parts" were corrected by Joseph Smith.

1869

The New Testament: Authorized Version Revised

This New Testament is the work of the Henry Alford (1810-1871) who collaborated with several others during the period of 1856-1861 to undertake a revision of the Authorized Version New Testament. He also produced several editions of the Greek New Testament. Although Alford utterly repudiated "for his Revision any aim to be adopted in any place as a substitute for the Authorized Version," he wished to "disabuse men's minds of the fallacies by which the Authorized Version is commonly defended." The work was based on the readings of "the now ascertained ancient Greek text."

1876

The Holy Bible

This translation by Julia Smith (1793-1886) is said to be "translated literally from the original tongues." She was a member of the Sandemanian sect founded in Scotland. She believed that the King James text "had not been given literally, and it was the literal meaning we were seeking." The order of books in the Old Testament has been changed and an attempt is made to give "the same English word for the same Hebrew or Greek word, everywhere."

CHAPTER FOUR

THE DELUGE

Although many attempts had been made to revise the Authorized Version since its inauguration in 1611, they were both personal and unauthorized. It was not until the publication of the Revised Version, whose New Testament was first released in 1881, that the dominance of the Authorized Version was seriously and officially challenged. Almost one new English translation per year was issued from the publication of the Revised Version to the modern era which begins with the Revised Standard Version New Testament in 1946. Since the deluge of English Bible translations that appear in this period began, not only with the Revised Version, but with the publication of a new edition of the Greek New Testament by Westcott and Hort, a review of the advancement and acceptance of the critical Greek text, and to a lesser extent, the Hebrew text, is indicative to put in perspective many of the modern versions of this period.

The Hebrew Old Testament

Up until this time, the Masoretic Text as found in the second Rabbinic Bible of Jacob ben Chayyim (1524-25) had been the standard Hebrew Old Testament text. Baer and Delitzsch attempted to reproduce the Masoretic text of the Old testament based on early manuscripts and editions. Their inconsequential work was issued in successive volumes from 1869 to 1892. Christian Ginsburg prepared an edition of the Hebrew Old Testament in 1894 based largely on Jacob ben Chayyim's Bible. Rudolph Kittel's *Biblia Hebraica*, which first appeared in 1906, was substantially the text of Chayyim. This foundation was also maintained in his second edition (1912). It was not until the third (1937) and subsequent editions of Kittel's *Biblia Hebraica*, based on the Leningrad Codex, that the traditional Masoretic Hebrew Old Testament text was abandoned.

The Greek New Testament

One of the most significant editions of the Greek New Testament ever published was that issued in 1881 by Brooke Foss Westcott (1825-1901) and Fenton John Anthony Hort (1828-1892). While the work of translating the Revised Version was in progress, Westcott and Hort were simultaneously engrossed in making their edition of the Greek New Testament. Successive installments of the text were privately furnished to the members of the translating committee. The Gospels were issued in 1871, the Acts in 1873, the General Epistles in 1873, the Pauline Epistles in 1875, and the Revelation in 1876. The completed edition appeared just five days before the Revised Version New Testament. It contained no critical apparatus, but a second volume published in 1882 contained an Introduction and Appendix that set forth the principles followed by Westcott and Hort in the preparation of their text. The Westcott and Hort text was vehemently opposed by Dean John William Burgon (1813-1888), as was the Revised Version. The Greek text underlying the Revised Version was also published in 1881. It was issued by Alexander Souter in 1910 containing a critical apparatus with a second edition appearing in 1947.

Other editions of the Greek New Testament soon followed. Another product of this period was *The Resultant Greek Testament* by Richard Weymouth (1822-1902). First issued in 1886, it was based on the readings of the majority of modern critical editions of the Greek New Testament. Weymouth issued two more editions in 1892 and 1905. Bernhard Weiss (1827-1918) brought forth two editions (1894-1900 and 1902-05) that were very similar to that of Westcott and Hort. Perhaps the most popular and enduring edition of the Greek New Testament was that of Eberhard Nestle (1851-1913), first published in 1898. He based his text on the majority reading of

Westcott and Hort, Tischendorf and Weymouth. Beginning with the third edition in 1901, Weiss was substituted for Weymouth. This text was adopted by the British and Foreign Bible Society in 1904, signifying the official end of the era of the Textus Receptus. The thirteenth edition, issued in 1927 and edited by Nestle's son Erwin, marks the beginning of the modern critical apparatus found in the recent Nestle editions. The seventeenth edition was released in 1941. A monumental edition of the Greek New Testament was issued in 1902-13 by Hermann von Soden (1852-1914). Three other editions of the Greek New Testament were prepared by Roman Catholic scholars: Heinrich Vogels in 1920 and 1922, Augustin Merk in 1933, and Jose Bover in 1943. These were all diglot editions, also containing the Latin Vulgate.

1881-1885

Revised Version

Although the translation of the Revised Version officially began with a resolution in 1870, which culminated in the publication of the New Testament in 1881, the impetus can be traced to the publication of several works in the years preceding it. In 1832 (re-edited in 1836 and 1849), there appeared the book *Hints for an Improved Translation of the New Testament* by James Scholefield, a professor of Greek at Cambridge. This was followed in 1856 by William Selwyn's *Notes on the proposed Amendment of the Authorized Version*. This in turn initiated Archbishop Trench's work in 1858: *On the Authorized Version of the New Testament, in connexion with some recent Proposals for its Revision*. Meanwhile, in 1856, five scholars, among them C.J. Ellicott and Henry Alford, agreed to privately undertake a revision of the Authorized Version New Testament beginning with the Gospel of John. This was issued in 1857 as *The Authorized Version of St John's Gospel, revised by Five Clergymen*. Subsequent translations of Romans and Corinthians appeared in 1858, while Galatians, Ephesians, and Philippians were issued in 1861. Alford later produced his own translation of the New Testament. As the work of the Revised Version was commencing, Ellicott brought forth *Considerations on the Revision of the English Version of the New Testament*, and in 1871, Lightfoot, one of the translators, added *On a Fresh Revision of the English New Testament*. In America, a volume edited by Philip Schaff appeared entitled *The Revision of the English Version of the New Testament*, which contained essays by Lightfoot, Trench, and Ellicott.

On February 10, 1870, Bishop Wilberforce introduced a motion to the Upper House of Convocation of the Province of Canterbury:

> That a Committee of both Houses be appointed, with power to confer with any Committee that may be appointed by the Convocation of the Northern Province, to report upon the desirableness of a revision of the Authorized Version of the New Testament, whether by marginal notes or otherwise, in all those passages where plain and clear errors, whether in the Hebrew or Greek text originally adopted by the translators, or in the translation made from the same, shall, on due investigation, be found to exist.

By an amendment, the Old Testament was included in this proposal. A committee was appointed, and on May 3, 1870, they issued a report consisting of five resolutions:

> 1. That it is desirable that a revision of the Authorized Version of the Holy Scriptures be undertaken.
> 2. That the revision be so conducted as to comprise both marginal renderings and such emendations as it may be found necessary to insert in the text of the Authorized Version.
> 3. That in the above resolutions we do not contemplate any new translation of the Bible, or any alteration of the language, except when in the judgment of the most competent scholars such change is necessary.
> 4. That in such necessary changes, the style of the language employed in the existing version be closely followed.
> 5. That it is desirable that Convocation should nominate a body of its own members to undertake the

work of revision, who shall be at liberty to invite the co-operation of any eminent for scholarship, to whatever nation or religious body they may belong.

These resolutions being adopted, another was proposed and approved:

> That a Committee be now appointed to consider and report to Convocation a scheme of revision on the principles laid down in the report now adopted, and that the Bishops of Winchester, St. David's, Llandaff, Gloucester and Bristol, Ely, Lincoln, and Bath and Wells, be members of the Committee. That the Committee be empowered to invite the co-operation of those whom they may judge fit from their Biblical Scholarship to aid them in their work.

A joint committee of sixteen then convened and separated into two companies, one for the Old Testament and one for the New. The Old Testament chairman was E.H. Brown and the New Testament was C.J. Ellicott. Invitations to become members of the Revision Committee were sent to the leading scholars of the day, including Trench, Hort, Lightfoot, Milligan, Moulton, Scrivener, and Westcott. Tregelles declined on account of failing health. The Roman Catholic, John Henry Newman, likewise dissented. A Unitarian, G. Vance Smith, also served on the committee.

The general principles to be followed during the work were eight in number:

> 1. To introduce as few alterations as possible into the Text of the Authorized Version consistently with faithfulness.
> 2. To limit, as far as possible, the expression of such alterations to the language of the Authorized and earlier English versions.
> 3. Each Company to go twice over the portion to be revised, once provisionally, the second time finally, and on principles of voting as hereinafter is provided.
> 4. That the Text to be adopted be that for which the

evidence is decidedly preponderating; and that when the Text so adopted differs from that from which the Authorized Version was made, the alteration be indicated in the margin.

5. To make or retain no change in the Text on the second final revision by each Company, except two-thirds of those present approve of the same, but on the first revision to decide by simple majorities.

6. In every case of proposed alteration that may have given rise to discussion, to defer the voting thereupon till the next Meeting, whensoever the same shall be required by one-third of those present at the Meeting, such intended vote to be announced in the notice for the next Meeting.

7. To revise the headings of chapters, pages, paragraphs, italics, and punctuation.

8. To refer, on the part of each Company, when considered desirable, to Divines, Scholars, and Literary men, whether at home or abroad, for their opinions.

The work on the New Testament began on June 22, 1870, with the Old Testament starting eight days later. The revisors of the New Testament met only for four days each month; the Old Testament revisors in ten-day secessions five times each year. In August of 1870, cooperation was sought from American biblical scholars including Timothy Dwight, Henry B. Smith, Matthew Riddle, and J. Henry Thayer. A committee was formed in December of 1871, and Dr. Woolsey was elected chairman of the New Testament and Dr. Green of the Old, while Philip Schaff was chosen president of the whole committee. Work actually began in October of the following year. Copies of the precursory revision finished by the English revisers were then circulated to the Americans for review.

The New Testament was published on May 17, 1881:

The New Testament of our Lord and Saviour Jesus Christ Translated out of the Greek: being the Version set forth A.D. 1611. Compared with the most ancient Authorities and Revised A.D. 1881. Printed for the Universities of Oxford and Cambridge. Oxford, at the University Press, 1881.

The English Revised New Testament was published in America on May 20 and the entire text was subsequently published in several newspapers. The Revised Version was immediately opposed in England by the textual scholar, Dean Burgon, in a series of articles for the *Quarterly Review* of 1881 and 1882. These articles were published in 1883 as *The Revision Revised*. Millions of copies, however, were still quickly sold in England and the United States.

The Old Testament was concluded four years later, and on May 19, 1885, the complete revised Bible was published:

> The Holy Bible Containing the Old and New Testaments. Translated out of the Original Tongues, Being the Version set forth A.D. 1611. Compared with the most ancient Authorities and Revised. Printed for the Universities of Oxford and Cambridge. Oxford, at the University Press, 1885.

After the arrival of the entire Revised Version, some of the revisers began work on the revision of the Apocrypha. It was made available in 1894 and bore its own title:

> The Apocrypha, Translated out of the Greek and Latin tongues; being the Version set forth A.D. 1611, Compared with the most ancient Authorities and Revised A.D. 1894. Oxford, at the University Press, 1894.

Although Westcott and Hort supplied to the Revision Committee the readings of their forthcoming Greek Testament, the New Testament text was an eclectic one. Not only were the various editions of the Received Text available, but also all the critical editions of Griesbach, Lachmann, Tischendorf, Alford, and Tregelles. The readings adopted by the revisers were published in the Oxford Greek Testament of 1881. The Old Testament revision was not as severe as the New since it was based on the same Massoretic Hebrew text as was the Authorized Version.

The Revised Version as a whole was characterized by a systematization and reduction of italicized words, a revision of punctuation, the omission of page and chapter headings, a listing of alternate renderings and variant readings in the margin, and sense paragraphs instead of verse paragraphs as in the Authorized Version. The revisers sought to use the same English word for each Greek word wherever possible. In their Preface to the New Testament, five types of alterations from the text of the Authorized Version are delineated: the adoption of a different underlying text, where the rendering seemed to be wrong, where the text was ambiguous, where the Authorized Version was inconsistent with itself in the renderings of two or more passages confessedly alike or parallel, and those rendered necessary by consequence of changes already made, although not in themselves required by the general rule of faithfulness.

1884

The Englishman's Bible

This complete work by Thomas Newberry was first issued as a New Testament in 1870. It aims to give the "accuracy, precision and certainty of the original hebrew and greek scriptures on the page of the authorized version." The text is divided into short paragraphs and arranged with dots, dashes, marginal analysis, and footnotes, all with the intent of giving more correct renderings of certain phrases.

1885

A Translation of the Old Testament Scriptures from the Original Hebrew

This translation, which is based on an unpointed Hebrew text, is the work of Helen Spurrell. She freely amended the text with the Samaritan Pentateuch and the Septuagint.

A New Translation

This is the completed work of John Nelson Darby (1800-1882), who was one of the founders of the Plymouth

Brethren movement. The New Testament was first issued in undated parts between 1859 and 1867, revised in 1871, with a third edition appearing in 1884. He also translated the Bible into French (1859) and German (1871), and it was on the basis of these editions that his full translation of the Bible was completed, since he died in 1882. The Old Testament was published in four parts between 1883 and 1885. A critical apparatus was included in the New Testament.

The New Covenant

This is a translation of the New Testament by the Universalist minister John Hanson. It was the first American translation to be based on the newly translated Greek text of Westcott and Hort. The four Gospels are printed as a Harmony while the remainder of the New Testament is in chronological order.

The Teaching and Acts of Jesus of Nazareth and His Apostles

This is a New Testament translated by W.D. Dillard. It claims to be "literally translated out of the Greek." The translator proposed to "render every word in the New Testament Greek into plain vernacular English words; just as they would now be written, if the facts they relate had occurred in our day and in our country."

1893

Scriptures, Hebrew and Christian

Issued in three volumes beginning in 1886, this translation contains "the words of the Bible, but with considerable condensation and rearrangement." The text somewhat follows the Authorized Version, but has been changed in the interests of simplifying passages or idioms with glosses and parentheses added. The Divine name is rendered as Jehovah throughout. The translators were John Peters and Edward Bartlett.

1897

The New Dispensation

Translated by Robert Weekes (1819-1898), this New Testament seeks "to ascertain, if possible, the thought of the writers, and then to express such thought correctly, in language which should be acceptable to both the ordinary reader and the scholar, with as little deviation from a literal rendering as practicable." The Westcott and Hort Greek text formed the basis for this translation, but it was not followed exclusively.

The New Testament Emphasized

This translation by Horace Morrow was "based upon a study of The Original Greek Text." Capital letters and italics were used to denote emphasis.

1898

American Revised Version

During the translating of the Revised Version, the American Committee had opportunity to review and remark on the work as undertaken by the English revisers. The revisers pledged to give "the most careful consideration" to the suggestions of the American Committee, but as the English had initiated the work, they had the determining vote on the final outcome. Suggestions made by the American committee were subject to the approval of two-thirds of the English group to be accepted. It was agreed that those readings proposed by the American committee and rejected, were to be recorded in an appendix to the Revised Version for a period of fourteen years. It was further acceded that the American committee, during this fourteen-year period, would recognize as authorized only those editions of the Revised Version that were approved by the University presses. An appendix was prepared that contained a minimum list of the American preferences in hope that they might ultimately be incorporated into the text. In 1881 and 1882, unauthorized editions incorporating these preferences into the Revised Version were published. In 1898, an official, authorized edition was published by Oxford and Cambridge Universities for the American market. It was referred to as the American Revised Bible.

The Woman's Bible

Produced exclusively by a group of women, this Bible was originally designed to revise only those passages "directly referring to women, and those also in which women are made prominent by exclusion." Nevertheless, the published work only contained selected texts presented with comments. The revising committee refers to another woman's Bible, that of Julia Smith in 1876, as their ultimate authority for the Hebrew and Greek.

1901

The Historical New Testament

This was the first translation effort of James Moffatt (1870-1944). This original translation arranged the biblical books in their chronological order and added a prolegomenon, tables, notes, and an appendix.

American Standard Version

The English revisers who produced the Revised Version disbanded their committee at the conclusion of their work. The American committee viewed the appendix to the Revised Version containing their preferences as "prepared under circumstances which rendered fulness and accuracy almost impossible." Therefore, the committee continued its work and resumed full activity in 1897. The leader of the American effort, Philip Schaff, died in 1893, and after other deaths and resignations, the committee was reduced to just nine in number. The Americans held their last committee meeting on April 19, 1900. After the expiration of the said fourteen-year period, the complete Bible was published on August 26, 1901:

The Holy Bible containing the Old and New Testaments translated out of the original tongues, being the version set forth A.D. 1611 compared with the most ancient authorities and revised A.D. 1881-1885. Newly Edited by the American Revision Committee A.D. 1901. Standard Edition. New York, Thomas Nelson & Sons.

The Bible was copyrighted and on the verso of the title page was the statement from which its name was drawn:

This Standard American Edition of the Revised Version of the Bible, and editions in conformity with it published by Messrs Thomas Nelson and Sons and certified by this endorsement, are the only editions authorized by the American Committee of Revision.

Unlike the English revisers, the Americans did not include the Apocrypha in their endeavor.

The changes made in the American Standard Version did not merely consist of transferring the readings of the Revised Version appendix to the text. Many of the alterations were "originally adopted by the American Old Testament Company at their second revision (and so by a two-thirds majority), but waived when the Appendix was prepared." Some renderings consist of a "return to the readings of the Authorized Version." Considerable attention was paid to the paragraph divisions and punctuation, as well as consistency throughout. Verse numbers were again displayed within the text. Where possible, certain changes were also "made for the sake of euphemism" since in modern times some terms "have become offensive." Furthermore, the general intention "to eliminate obsolete, obscure, and misleading terms" from the Authorized Version has "been more fully carried out." Other specific corrections were made "which have seemed to be required by regard for pure English idiom."

The Modern American Bible

This New Testament is the work of Frank Ballentine (1859-1936). It was released in parts beginning in 1899 and was based on the Textus Receptus and the later Greek texts.

1902

Twentieth Century New Testament

This translation began with a tentative edition in 1898. It arose because of what was thought to be "difficult, or even quite unintelligible" passages in the King James Version. The work is based on the Greek text of Westcott and Hort. The translators were an ecumenical group that included housewives, businessmen, and schoolteachers. One peculiar feature found in this work is the change in the order of the books of the New Testament. A revised edition was issued in 1904 as well as a Moody reprint in 1961 that restores the traditional order of books and makes some further changes in the text.

The Emphasized Bible

Previously published as just a New Testament in 1872 and 1878, this is the complete work of Joseph Rotherham (1828-1910). The first two editions were based on the text of Tregelles, but this has now been superseded by the text of Westcott and Hort. The Old Testament was based on the revised text of Ginsburg. This Bible is "emphasized" in that it uses indentations, varieties of type, headings, footnotes, and references to indicate various shades of emphasis in the original text. One of the main points of this translation is to "restore" the Tetragrammaton to its proper form of Yahweh instead of Jehovah or Lord. In summary, it is a translation "designed to set forth the exact meaning, the proper terminology, and the graphic style of the sacred original."

Translation of the New Testament from the Original Greek

This translation by W.B. Godbey (1833-1920) was based on Tischendorf's edition of Codex Sinaiticus, although he did not follow the order of books.

1903

The New Testament in Modern Speech

This is the translation of the New Testament by Richard Weymouth (1822-1902). In 1886, Weymouth first published *The Resultant Greek Testament,* his own edition of the Greek New Testament, and then began his translation based on it. He claimed that it was not his "ambition to supplant the Versions already in general use." Considerable attention was given to "the exact rendering of the tenses of the Greek verb." Weymouth died before it was published, but it was then issued as edited by Ernest Hampden-Cook. A second edition appeared in 1904, and numerous other editions followed.

The Holy Bible in Modern English

This complete Bible originally appeared as a New Testament in 1895. It is the work of Ferrar Fenton in which he sought to make the Scriptures "clearly intelligible" by being "translated absolutely afresh from the Hebrew and Greek into the same style and diction as all our current literature." Fenton contends that his work "is the most accurate rendering into any European language, ancient or modern, ever made." He believed he was the only man "who has ever applied real mental and literary criticism to the Sacred Scriptures."

1904

The New Testament Revised and Translated

This New Testament, which was translated by Adolphus Worrell (1831-1908), makes the claim that it approaches to "far greater fidelity to the original Greek" than most others. Special attention has been given to the proper translation of the Greek tenses. The translator introduces the book "in the interest of no denomination," but expects it to be appreciated by "intelligent Christians." The work was based on the 1881 Greek text of Westcott and Hort.

The Corrected English New Testament

Believing that the Revised Version was a "failure," Samuel Lloyd began work on this New Testament in 1901. He sought to correct "without defacing" the Authorized Version by removing defects and revising the English so as to "give the presentday reader a freer access to the meaning, and a higher appreciation of the literary quality of the Greek." The work was based on the 1904 edition of Nestle's Greek text.

1907

The Modern Reader's Bible

Edited by Richard Moulton (1849-1924) and originally released in twenty-one volumes beginning in 1895, this Bible also includes three books of the Apocrypha. It attempts to investigate "the exact literary form and detailed structure of the books of Scripture; and then to use all the devices of modern printing for the purpose of indicating such structure to the eye of the reader." The order of biblical books has been rearranged under various literary forms. The text is based on the Revised Version, but with certain changes made to adapt the Bible to "modern literary structure."

1909

The Bible in Modern English

This New Testament is a revision of the Modern American Bible of 1901 by Frank Ballentine. It claims to be "a rendering from the originals by an American making use of the best scholarship and latest researches at home and abroad."

1911

The 1911 Tercentenary Commemoration Bible

Issued to commemorate the 300th year since the Authorized

Version was first published, this revision of the Authorized Version introduced moderate corrections and improvements to the text. The reason was explained as: "It was felt, however, that in preparing an edition commemorative of this unique event occasion might fitly be found for a careful scrutiny of the text with a view of correction in the light of the best modern research such passages as are misleading or needlessly obscure." It is claimed that the text of this edition was carefully scrutinized by a "committee of 34 eminent Hebrew and Greek scholars, representing all of the great evangelical bodies and many foremost Universities and Schools of Divinity." This work profess to be "neither a new translation nor revision, but a scholarly and carefully Corrected Text."

1912

The Holy Bible: An Improved Edition

This Bible was originally the attempt of the American Bible Union to produce an "immersionist" version. The New Testament was published in a single edition in 1864. This was then revised several times and then released with the Old Testament in 1912. The distinguishing characteristic of this version is the double rendering of "baptize (immerse)" whenever the ordinance is mentioned. Words that appear in italics in the Authorized Version are here printed in Roman type or occasionally put in brackets. The poetic form is used for Job, Psalms, Proverbs, and much of the Prophets. Alternative renderings are also provided in the notes.

1914

The New Covenant

This is a revision of the Authorized Version by E.E. (Edward) Cunnington. The translator was prompted to make his translation because of his dissatisfaction with the Revised Version, of which he states: "it is little to say that it has not closed the door upon other attempts."

The New Testament from the Greek text as establish by Bible Numerics

This is the work of Ivan Panin (1855-1942). He claimed to have discovered a mathematical design underlying the Greek text of the New Testament and on this basis made his own translation into English. The author states that "the standard used for comparison was: for the Greek, the Revision of Westcott & Hort; and, for the English, the American Revised Version."

1916

The Historical Bible

This six-volume set was begun in 1909. It contains a condensed paraphrase by Charles Kent (1867-1925), and was one of many attempts by the author at Bible translating.

1917

The Holy Scriptures According to the Masoretic Text

This is a Jewish Version of the Old Testament by the Jewish Publication Society. It is the first translation "for which a group of men representative of Jewish learning among English-speaking Jews assume joint responsibility." The translators aspire to "combine the spirit of Jewish tradition with the results of biblical scholarship, ancient, medieval, and modern." A determining factor in the translation was that "the christological interpretations in non-Jewish translations are out of place in a Jewish Bible." Therefore, "The Jew cannot afford to have his Bible translation prepared for him by others."

1918

The New Testament

This translation was prepared by Henry Anderson and is a major revision of his earlier effort (1864) based on the recently discovered Codex Sinaiticus. It was published posthumously.

1919

The Messages of the Bible

Jointly edited by Frank Sanders and Charles Kent, this Bible is arranged chronologically and is actually a paraphrase.

1921

The Shorter Bible

The New Testament of this Bible was published in 1918. Charles Kent translated and arranged this work with the help of four other editors. It is an abridgment with about two-thirds of the Old Testament and one-third of the New Testament being omitted.

1923

The Riverside New Testament

This translation by William Ballantine (1848-1937) is from an eclectic rendering of Nestle's text and avers to translate the "original Greek into the English of today." There are no verse numbers, references, or notes. It underwent a revision in 1934.

1924

Centenary Translation of the New Testament

So called because it marked the first hundred years of the work of the American Baptist Publication Society, this version was the work of Helen Montgomery (1861-1934). It is also called The New Testament in Modern English. The translator aims to "offer a translation in the language of everyday life, that does not depart too much from the translations already familiar and beloved." This version intends "to remove the veil that a literary or formal translation inevitable puts between the reader of only average education and the meaning of the text." It was based on the Greek text underlying the Revised Version.

The Everyday Bible

This work by Charles Sheldon (1857-1946), which was edited over a twenty-five year period, is an abridgment of the American Standard Version that omits the Levitical Laws, genealogies, and parts of the prophecies. There are no chapter or verse divisions.

1925

The People's New Covenant

This New Testament was translated "from the Meta-Physical standpoint." It is supposedly "unhampered by so-called Ecclesiastical authority." This version "recognizes healing as well as teaching as a component part of true Christianity" and is based on the premise of "Scientific Statement of Being" as given in the writings of Mary Baker Eddy. The translator and publisher was Arthur Overbury.

1926

The Holy Bible: A New Translation

This is the second work of James Moffatt. The New Testament first appeared in 1913 based on the Greek text of von Soden. A revised edition appeared in 1917. The Old Testament was published in 1924-25. The complete Bible, first issued in 1926, was revised again in 1935. Moffatt claimed that his work was "a fresh translation of the original, not a revision of any English version." He intended to "present the books of the Old and New Testament in effective, intelligible English." He sought to translate the Bible as he would any other book. Certain verses, and in some cases whole chapters, have been transposed and many conjectural emendations are adopted. Moffatt regarded the traditional text as "often desperately corrupt."

Concordant Version

The translator, A.E. Knoch, began work on this New Testament in 1914. It was issued in installments until the completed version in 1926. A major revision followed in 1931. This translation claims that it is "the only one which practically acknowledges the inspiration or vitality of the Sacred Scriptures." The objective of this version is "to go to the very limits of fidelity in translating the word of God into English." This is accomplished by "uniformity and consistency" in translation. Each Greek word is uniformly translated by the same English word. Where uniformity is impractical, consistency is observed in the use of synonyms. Hence the reason it is called the Concordant Version: the rendering for each word is concordant or in agreement every time. The Greek text used was the Resultant Greek Testament of Weymouth, although this was freely corrected with "ancient manuscripts."

1927

The Student's Old Testament

Issued in six volumes beginning in 1904, this translation by Charles Kent rearranges the writings of the Old Testament in a logical order and seeks "to introduce the reader by means of a clear translation to the beauty and thought of the original."

1928

The Christian's Bible: New Testament

The translator and publisher of this version was George LeFevre. The basis of the translation was Codex Sinaiticus and Codex Vaticanus.

The Living Bible

This Bible edited by Bolton Hall (1854-1938) attempted "to present in condensed form the entire contents of the Scriptures, omitting only repetitions, ceremonial details, most genealogies, land-boundaries, and matter that is no longer of general interest." It aims to be the whole Bible "in its fewest words."

1931

The Complete Bible: An American Translation

This Bible contains the 1923 New Testament translation of Edgar Goodspeed (1871-1962) and the 1927 Old Testament translation of J.M. Powis Smith and others. Later editions beginning in 1939 included the Apocrypha as translated by Goodspeed. The intent of the translators was to produce a new translation "based upon the assured results of modern study, and put in the familiar language of today." The Greek text followed for the New Testament was that of Westcott and Hort.

1933

The Short Bible

This abridgment contains the books of the Bible arranged chronologically with selections from each book. However, some books are omitted completely. The purpose of this version of the Bible is to "present those parts of it which everyone ought to be acquainted with, from a literary, historical, or religious point of view." It uses as its text the 1923 Goodspeed New Testament and the 1927 Smith Old Testament.

1934

The Documents of the New Testament

This translation by G.W. Wade arranges the biblical books in chronological order. It claims to be accurate, yet not literal rendering of what is substantially the text of Westcott and Hort. The translation is expanded by the use of italics and includes various aids to those beginning to study New Testament documents.

1935

The Westminster Version of the Sacred Scriptures

Although not an official Roman Catholic translation, this New Testament was the work of Catholic scholars. Work was begun on this version in 1913. It contains extensive introductions and comments. A small edition with the complete text but only brief introductions was published in 1948. Several books of the Old Testament were later completed and published, but the Bible as a whole never came to fruition.

1937

The New Testament in the Language of the People

This is the work of Charles B. Williams. At the time of its publication, it was claimed to be "the best translation of the New Testament existing in the English language today." Important attention was given to the Greek tenses. The translator's aim was to "make this greatest book in the world readable and understandable by the plain people." Practical everyday words are used to replace "technical religious and theological terms." The emphasis in this version is on the thoughts of the New Testament, "not its single words." The work was based on the Westcott and Hort Greek text but followed the Vatican manuscript when faced with conflicting variants.

The New Testament of our Lord and Saviour Jesus Christ

This work by Francis Spencer is one of the earlier attempts by a Roman Catholic to render an English translation directly from the original languages instead of the Latin. As the translator stated: "The Vulgate, the authentic text of the Latin Church, retains all its authority in the official acts of that Church; but it is desirable to have a translation from the original languages which avails itself of the assured results and the progress of textual criticism." The Gospels were originally released in 1901 and the final product was finished before Spencer's death in 1913, although it was not published at that time. The manuscript was edited for publication by Charles Callan and John McHugh and published in 1937. The text is printed in paragraphs with the verse numbers in the margin. The words of Christ are in italics and quotations from the Old Testament appear in small capitals.

The New Testament: A New Translation and Explanation

This translation was originally made in German by Johannes Greber, a former Roman Catholic priest who came to believe in communication with the world of divine spirits. He based his translation on Codex Bezae which he claimed "most nearly approaches the truth" and sought to "reproduce the exact meaning of the Greek text." He freely acknowledged that he employed readings not found in any manuscripts on the basis of "the divine spirits." The translation of his German original into English was made by a professional translator, and subsequently corrected and revised by Americans.

1941

The Confraternity Version

So called because it was sponsored by the Episcopal Committee of the Confraternity of Christian Doctrine, this Roman Catholic New Testament is a revision of the Challoner-Rheims New Testament. It possesses "the authority necessary in any serious attempt to meet the requirements of an improved Catholic version in English." Where it departs from the Challoner-Rheims, "the Clementine edition of the Vulgate is the main source." A few earlier readings have been incorporated which "tends to bring the text basic to the present version very close to the modern critical editions of the original Greek."

CHAPTER FIVE

THE MARKETPLACE

The last milestone in the history of English translations of the Bible was the publication in 1946 of the New Testament of the controversial Revised Standard Version. This ushers in our modern age where not only are so many versions available, but competition abounds in the marketplace for sales and readership. Although many modern translations have appeared since the publication of the Revised Version and the American Standard Version, the arrival of the Revised Standard Version offered the first major challenge to the domination of the Authorized Version since then. At the present time, the much heralded Revised Version and American Standard Version can scarcely be found and the Revised Standard Version is perhaps the oldest major English translation readily available besides the Authorized Version. Also in this period, new editions of Kittle's *Biblia Hebraica* have appeared. The 7th edition of 1951 includes variants of the Dead Sea scrolls. More significantly, there have also been published new editions of the Greek New Testament, which will be surveyed directly, since in many cases they are the foundation for new translations of the Bible.

The Greek New Testament

In this modern period of English Bible translations, there stands out the continued publication of editions of Nestle's *Novum Testamentum Graece*. The 20th edition appeared in 1950. The 21st edition saw the addition of Kurt Aland as editor with Erwin Nestle. Other editions followed in 1956, 1959, 1960, and 1963. The present edition is the 26th, and includes as editors Kurt Aland, Matthew Black, Carlo Martini, Bruce Metzger, and

Allen Wikgren.

Bover, Merk, and Vogels continued to produce editions of their Greek New Testaments, but they are of little influence. After the publication in 1961 of the New Testament of the New English Bible, an edition of the Greek text that embodies that version was issued in 1964 by R. Tasker, a member of the Panel of Translators.

The dominant text for translators during this period was first published in 1966 as *The Greek New Testament*. Originally sponsored by the American Bible Society, and joined later by the Scottish, Dutch, British and Foreign, and Wurttemberg Bible Societies, it is now published under the auspices of the United Bible Societies. It is also distributed by the Roman Catholic Church. *The Greek New Testament* was the result of a decade of research by five international scholars: Kurt Aland, Matthew Black, Bruce Metzger, Allen Wikgren, and Arthur Voobus. It is sometimes referred to as the "Aland and Metzger" text. The second edition of 1968 saw the replacement of Voobus with Carlo Martini, a Roman Catholic cardinal. A third edition was published in 1975 which was reproduced exactly in the 26th edition of the Nestle-Aland text, differing only in paragraphing, orthography, punctuation, and the critical apparatus. A fourth edition is in the works at this present time.

Throughout this period, the Trinitarian Bible Society continued to publish the Textus Receptus or Received Text. In 1982, a new type of text made its appearance: *The Greek New Testament According to the Majority Text*, edited by Arthur Farstad and Zane Hodges. A second edition was issued in 1985. A rival Majority Text edited by Maurice Robinson and William Pierpont was published in 1991: *The New Testament in the Original Greek According to the Byzantine/Majority Textform*. No translations thus far are based upon either edition of the Majority Text.

1948

The Letchworth Version in Modern English

This New Testament by T.F. Ford and R.E. Ford is basically that of the Authorized Version with an attempt to substitute modern English for what was deemed archaic words and phrases. It originates from Letchworth in England, hence the name.

1949

The Bible in Basic English

This Bible, originally released as a New Testament in 1941, is from the Cambridge University Press and employs the Basic English developed by C.K. Ogden of the Orthological Institute in England. Basic English professes to be "a simple form of the English language which, with 850 words, is able to give the sense of anything which may be said in English." To this was added 150 more words "for the purpose of putting the Bible into Basic." This translation is not a rendering of any other into Basic English, but is a fresh translation from the Hebrew and Greek "designed to be used wherever the English language has taken root." An American edition was issued in 1950.

1950

The Dartmouth Bible

So called because its editors were working on behalf of Dartmouth College, this edition of the Bible is not a new translation but an abridgment of the King James Version. The editors state that many of its inherent defects "have been overcome by the abridgment." About one-half of the total text is omitted. The advisory board, and others who aided in the work, consisted of an ecumenical group of professors, clergy, and laymen. This abridgment supposedly "omits only passages which are repetitive or of little interest to those who are not technical students." The Apocrypha is also included.

1951

The Authentic Version

The translator of this New Testament believed that he had

"been given divine authority through the Holy Spirit to bring the true translation of the original Greek text." He further claimed that his translation was "compared with the original Greek text by the use of the best Greek dictionaries and former translations."

1952

Revised Standard Version

As previously mentioned, the New Testament was first published in 1946. This translation claims to be an "authorized revision of the American Standard Version, published in 1901, which was a revision of the King James Version, published in 1611." The copyright of the American Standard Version was acquired in 1928 by the International Council of Religious Education (now connected with the National Council of Churches). The Council appointed a committee, which voted in 1937 to authorize a new revision which would embody "the best results of modern scholarship as to the meaning of the Scriptures" while expressing "this meaning in English diction which is designed for use in public and private worship and preserves those qualities which have given to the King James Version a supreme place in English literature."

The Revised Standard Version was produced by thirty-two scholars from various denominations including a Jewish professor. Luther Weigle served as chairman while James Moffatt, Edgar Goodspeed, and J.M. Powis Smith, the three of which each produced earlier translations, also collaborated. The completed Bible was published on September 30, 1952, and the Apocrypha was translated later. Some changes were incorporated into the text of the previously released New Testament when the completed Bible was published. In 1962, the Revised Standard Version was again slightly revised. In 1966, a Catholic edition appeared with the Apocrypha included as an integral part of the Old Testament and some minor changes in the New Testament. The official second edition of the Revised Standard Version New Testament was issued in 1971.

The Old Testament was based on the traditional Hebrew text with corrections from the ancient versions and the Qumran texts.

Variants have been settled by "the best judgment of competent scholars." The New Testament text is an eclectic one, although the final readings can, for the most part, be found in the text or margin of Nestle's 17th edition. The King James Version is claimed to have "grave defects," and the Greek text upon which it was based is said to be "marred by mistakes, containing the accumulated errors of fourteen centuries of manuscript copying." In brief, "The Revised Standard Version is not a new translation in the language of today. It is not a paraphrase which aims at striking idioms. It is a revision which seeks to preserve all that is best in the English Bible as it has been known and used through the years."

The New Testament: A New Translation in Plain English

This translation is by Charles K. Williams, not to be confused with Charles B. Williams, the translator of The New Testament in the Language of the People. It was based on the Greek text of Souter. "Plain English" is a simplified form of the English language based on 1,500 words that make up ordinary English speech. Any additional words that were used were explained in a glossary. The translation is characterized by short sentences. Certain words have been "changed or omitted to suit modern English usage."

1953

The New Testament: A New, Independent, Individual Translation

George Moore, the translator, states: "The reason for this translation is that I want to do it, that there is none that exactly suits me, and, since it is absolutely mine, and mine only, independent, individual, unsponsored, and dedicated solely to accuracy, clarity, and simplicity, it is possible that it may induce more individuals to read the Scriptures." The Greek text used was the 1950 Oxford University edition. Moore sought to "achieve an English text that anybody with a grade school education can read and understand."

1954

The New Testament Rendered From the Original Greek

This is a private Roman Catholic translation into modern, popular English from the 1943 edition of the Greek text of Bover. The translators were James Kleist (1873-1949) and Joseph Lilly (1893-1952).

1955

The Authentic New Testament

This is the work of Hugh Schonfield, a Jewish scholar. He professes to be "the first Jew to translate the New Testament into English." He further explains that the title *The Authentic New Testament* "relates to the quality of the New Testament itself." This version was based on "a critical text, arrived at by a painstaking study of copies and versions." Verse numberings are eliminated and the order of books has been rearranged.

The Holy Bible: A Translation from the Latin Vulgate

This is a Roman Catholic translation by Ronald Knox (1888-1957). It was based on the Latin Clementine Vulgate of 1592, although it was translated "in the light of the Hebrew and Greek originals." The New Testament was first published separately in 1945 after being issued privately by subscription in 1944. The Old Testament first appeared in two volumes in 1949.

1957

The Holy Bible from Ancient Eastern Manuscripts

This is George Lamsa's translation from the Aramaic of the Peshitta. The New Testament first appeared in 1940. Lamsa is an Assyrian and a native of the Bible lands. The publisher relates that Lamsa's background and knowledge of the Aramaic language enable him "to recover much of the meaning that has been lost in other translation of the Scriptures." Lamsa contends that "the Gospels, as well as the Epistles, were written in Aramaic." He believes that his translation "will throw considerable light on many obscure passages and that it will elucidate many other passages which have lost their meaning because of mistranslations."

1958

The New Testament in Modern English

Previously published in four parts beginning in 1947, this is the translation by J.B. Phillips. The translator sought to imagine himself "as each of the New Testament authors writing his particular message for the people of today." Phillips acknowledges that "consistency and meticulous accuracy have sometimes both been sacrificed in the attempt to transmit freshness and life across the centuries." The translation was supposedly made "from the best available Greek text."

1959

The Holy Bible: The Berkeley Version in Modern English

Originally released in 1945 as The Berkeley Version of the New Testament, this Bible was so named because the translator lived in Berkeley, California. Gerrit Verkuyl was the translator of the New Testament and served as editor of the Old Testament. The New Testament was based on the eighth edition of Tischendorf's Greek text although other texts were consulted. The traditional text of the Old Testament is sometimes amended with the Dead Sea Scrolls or the Septuagint.

1960

The Children's "King James" Bible: New Testament

This is one of the first works by Jay Green. It is a modern version based on the King James Version.

1961

The New Testament: An Expanded Translation

This New Testament is the work of Kenneth Wuest that previously appeared in three parts beginning with the Gospels in 1956. It differs from standard translations in that it "uses as many English words as are necessary to bring out the richness, force, and clarity of the Greek text." Significance is placed on the Greek order of words, the distinctions between Greek synonyms, the action found in Greek tenses, the use of Greek personal pronouns and the presence or absence of the definite article. This translation "attempts to bring out the full meaning of each Greek word" while holding "very closely to the earliest and most accurate Greek texts." It was based on Nestle's text with help from the standard Greek grammars and word studies.

Simplified New Testament in Plain English

This translation of the New Testament is the product of Olaf Norlie. It is supposed to be "a new translation from the original Greek designed to make the language of the New Testament more interesting and intelligible." It aims to use simple words and short sentences. It is designed "especially for today's young people who are not familiar with many of the obscure, archaic and complicated terms used in other and older versions." A new translation of the Psalms by R.K. Harrison is included.

New World Translation

Originally released in six volumes from 1950 to 1960, this version was produced by the Watchtower Bible and Tract Society and is known today as the Jehovah's Witness Bible. The second revision was published in 1970, the third in 1971, and the fourth in 1984. The translators "fear and love the Divine Author of the Holy Scriptures" and "feel a responsibility toward the searching readers who depend upon a translation of the inspired Word of the most High God for their everlasting salvation."

1962

Teen-age Version

This translation was prepared by Jay P. Green because "every teen-ager wants everything he owns to be peculiarly his or her own." This Bible has "easy-to-understand language," yet "a definite word-for-word treatment of the original Greek and Hebrew has been given. No rewriting of God's holy words has been attempted. There has been no tampering, paraphrasing, or improvement of God's Scriptures."

1963

The New Testament in the Language of Today

This translation by William Beck relies on recently discovered papyri and "other fine manuscripts" to "make this an accurate New Testament." It aims to put the Greek of the New Testament in "the living language of today."

1965

The Amplified Bible

First released as a New Testament in 1958, this version was produced by a committee of twelve editors for the Lockman Foundation. The Amplified Bible "amplifies" the text by supplying alternative renderings or additional words to clarify "shades of meaning that may be concealed." It is maintained that "possibly for the first time the full meaning of the key words in the original text is available in an English version of the Bible." The translation was based on the Westcott and Hort Greek text.

1966

Jerusalem Bible

This is the first Roman Catholic translation to be made

directly from the original languages instead of the Latin Vulgate. This Bible is the English counterpart of the French published in 1956. Although not translated from the French, the French version was consulted "where questions of variant reading or interpretation arose." The language used is "contemporary."

1967

New Scofield Reference Bible

This version claims that it is not "a new translation," but a revision of the Scofield Bible of 1917. However, not just the Scofield notes have been changed. The text continues to be the King James Version, "but with certain word changes." A committee convened over a ten year period to change obsolete and archaic words, words that have altered their meaning, indelicate words or expressions, proper names, and incorrect translations in the King James Version. Obsolete spelling has also been brought up to date. The committee declares its "adherence to the authority of the infallible Word of God in respect to both faith and practice."

1969

Modern Language Bible

This is a new edition of the 1959 Berkeley Version. The Old Testament has been updated and improved and the New Testament has undergone a major revision. It claims to be "a complete translation of every word in the Bible." Doubtful readings are placed in brackets.

The New Testament: A New translation

Published in two volumes, with the first appearing in 1968, this translation is the work of William Barclay. His admitted two aims were "to try to make the New Testament intelligible to the man who is not a technical scholar" and "to try to make a translation which did not need a commentary to explain it."

The Greek text used was the United Bible Societies 1966 edition. To make the Pauline Epistles "clearer," long sentences are broken up and periodically an expanded translation is given. Difficult passages have on occasion had explanations incorporated and integrated into the text "for the sake of clarity." The order of the Epistles has also been altered.

The Children's New Testament

This translation of the New Testament is the work of Gleason Ledyard. The translator gives the reason for his work as to "take difficult words that are found in most translations of the Bible and put them into words or phrases that are easy to understand." Only about 850 different words have been used in the making of this version. Significant features include "concise sentence structure, an understandable vocabulary, and short paragraphing." Upon completion, The Children's New Testament was "read and approved by New Testament and Greek scholars for accuracy and clarity."

1970

New English Bible

The New Testament of this version was first published in 1961. A second edition of the New Testament, incorporating some minor changes, together with the newly translated Old   •
Testament, was introduced in 1970. It is available with or without the Apocrypha. It purports to be "not a revision of any previous version," but made "direct from the original languages into contemporary English." The Old Testament basis for the work was the 1937 edition of Kittel's *Biblia Hebraica* with deviations based on the Dead Sea Scrolls, the Septuagint, and other ancient versions. The order of some verses in the Old Testament has been changed and the headings of the Psalms have been omitted. The New Testament was translated on the eclectic principle, with the translators selecting "the reading which in their judgement seemed most likely to represent what the author wrote." The resulting Greek text was published

separately in 1964 as *The Greek New Testament.*

New American Bible

This is the first American Roman Catholic translation made from the Hebrew and Greek instead of the Latin. This work originally began as The Confraternity Version in 1941. However, after the publication of the New Testament, work on the Old Testament was begun from the Hebrew, instead of just being a revision like the New Testament. Upon completion of the Old Testament, the New Testament was freshly translated from the Greek. The Greek text used was Nestle's 25th edition with additional help from the United Bible Societies' text of 1966. However, the editors "did not confine themselves strictly to these texts." Readings that were regarded "doubtful" appear in brackets while "poorly attested readings do not occur in this translation." This translation is the work of some fifty scholars, many of whom are not Catholic.

The Restoration of Original Sacred Name Bible

This translation is based on the Rotherham translation. It claims to be "restoring into the Scriptures the sacred glorious Name of the Heavenly Father and His Son." God the Father is now Yahvah, while Jesus Christ is now Yahshua. Since God has only "one name," this new translation of the Bible seeks to transliterate or transfer it "from Hebrew into whatever language is desired." The responsible party for this version is the Missionary Dispensary Bible Research.

King James II Version

This is another in a series of translations by Jay P. Green. It was based on the same texts as the King James Version and is "translated word-for-word in an attempt to give a literal rendition of each and every one of God's words." The language is affirmed to be "easy-to-understand" yet "a strong effort has been made to keep all the majesty, beauty and glory" of the original King James Version. A slightly revised edition was released twice in 1971.

.

1971

The Living Bible

Translated solely by Kenneth Taylor, this is a paraphrase based on the American Standard Version of 1901. It was previously published in installments beginning with Living Letters in 1962. It has also appeared in many forms such as Reach Out, The Way, and The Book. The translator maintains that his work "has undergone several major manuscript revisions and has been under the careful scrutiny of a team of Greek and Hebrew experts to check content, and of English critics for style." Taylor's stated purpose was "to say as exactly as possible what the writers of the Scripture meant, and to say it simply, expanding where necessary for a clear understanding by the modern reader." He does acknowledge, however, that "there are dangers in paraphrases, as well as values."

New American Standard Bible

First published as a New Testament in 1963, this is another translation produced by the Lockman Foundation. The fifty-eight anonymous translators were an ecumenical group from many different denominations. This version is supposed to be an update of the American Standard Version of 1901. The Lockman Foundation "felt an urgency to update it by incorporating recent discoveries of Hebrew and Greek textual sources and by rendering it into more current English." Numerous other translations were consulted along with "the linguistic tools and literature of biblical scholarship." The translation aims to render the Greek into "contemporary English." The latest edition of Kittel's *Biblia Hebraica* was employed for the Old Testament while the New Testament was based on the Greek text of Nestle's 23rd edition with consideration "given to the latest available manuscripts." Careful attention was given to the proper translation of the Greek tenses. Minor changes have been incorporated into the text over the years.

1972

The New Testament in Modern English

This is the revised edition of J.B. Phillips New Testament which appeared in 1958. Phillips insists that it is "in fact a new translation" and that "every single Greek word was read and considered." The translation was based on what Phillips considered "the latest and best Greek text" published by the United Bible Societies in 1966.

The Bible in Living English

This translation by Steven Byington was published by the Watchtower Bible and Tract Society, although the translator was not a Jehovah's Witness. His stated purpose was to "put the Bible into living present-day English." The name of God is rendered "Jehovah," hence the reason for the publication of this translation.

1973

Translator's New Testament

Published by the British and Foreign Bible Society, this translation is designed to "make available, to those translators of the New Testament into their own mother tongue who depend on English for access to the sources of biblical scholarship, such help as is necessary for the making of effective translations in the language of today." It is a specialized work for Bible translators based on the United Bible Societies' Greek text of 1966.

Cotton Patch Version

Beginning with the Pauline Epistles in 1968, this New Testament is the work of Clarence Jordan. He sought to "have the good news come to us not only in our own tongue but in our own time." It is an attempt to translate "not only the words but the events." These goals are achieved by taking the locations of the New Testament events and transferring them to the Southeastern United States. Jordan admits that his "attempts to find present-day equivalents to many new Testament expressions and concepts are often strained, crude and perhaps even inaccurate."

Common Bible

This ecumenical edition of the Revised Standard Version is endorsed by Roman Catholics, Greek Orthodox, and Protestants. It includes, in two appendixes, the Deuterocanonical books, and 1 and 2 Esdras and the Prayer of Manasseh. The Greek additions to Esther are placed within the Hebrew narrative.

1974

The New Testament in Everyday English

The translator of this work is Don Klingensmith. Westcott and Hort was the primary Greek text used with references to Nestle's as well. The translation attempts to use only the simple words of everyday English. The chapter and verse divisions are also omitted.

1976

An American Translation

First released in 1963 as The New Testament in the Language of Today, this is the completed Bible by William Beck. His goal was to "have God talk to the hearts of people in their language of today and tomorrow." Beck claims to "go farther than any other translation." He further maintained that his Bible was "the most accurate on the market, in regard to the best text, the most thorough lexicographical, grammatical, and archeological evidence."

Good News Bible

This was originally published as a New Testament in 1966

as Good News for Modern Man: The New Testament in Today's English Version. The translator of the New Testament was Robert Bratcher of the American Bible Society. It went through three editions with the forth edition being combined with the Old Testament to make the Good News Bible. The concern of the translators was to "provide a faithful translation of the meaning of the Hebrew, Aramaic, and Greek texts." They stated their first task as to "understand correctly the meaning of the original" Secondly, they tried to "express that meaning in a manner and form easily understood by the readers" in language that is "natural, clear, simple, and unambiguous." The Old Testament was based on Kittel's *Biblia Hebraica* (3rd edition, 1937). Variant readings, ancient versions, and conjectural emendations were employed when deemed necessary. The New Testament was based on the texts of the United Bible Societies, but in a few instances the translation "is based on a variant reading supported by one or more Greek manuscripts."

1977

The Christian Counselor's New Testament

This New Testament is the work of Jay Adams. It has been designed "as a working tool that may be used during counseling sessions" through the addition of "a system of highlighting, together with marginal notations and explanatory and applicatory footnotes." The translation itself is also the product of Jay Adams because he just "was not fully satisfied with the translations that were available."

1978

The Simple English Bible

This Bible is actually just a New Testament. It avows to use "only easy phrase structures and a vocabulary of about three thousand words." The claim is also made that The Simple English Bible translation "may be the most useful one for a majority of English speakers." The Greek text followed was an eclectic one, relying on Westcott and Hort, Nestle's 25th edition, the United Bible Societies' 3rd edition, and others. Painstaking effort was exercised "not to deviate from the best available Greek manuscripts."

New International Version

First released as a New Testament in 1973, the original name for this version was A Contemporary Translation. Over 100 international scholars from many different denominations worked "directly from the best available Hebrew, Aramaic and Greek texts" to produce this version under sponsorship of the New York International Bible Society. "Stylistic consultants" were employed since "a sensitive feeling for style does not always accompany scholarship." It is asserted that "no other translation has been made by a more thorough process of review and revision from committee to committee than this one." The Old Testament follows the latest editions of *Biblia Hebraica* with corrections from the Samaritan Pentateuch, ancient scribal traditions, Hebrew variants, the Targums, the Septuagint, Symmachus, Theodotion, the Dead Sea Scrolls, and the Vulgate. The New Testament text was an eclectic one based on "the best current printed texts of the Greek New Testament." Variants have been decided "according to accepted principles of New Testament textual criticism. Changes deemed necessary from the first published New Testament have been incorporated into the text of the complete Bible.

1979

The New Testament in Everyday English

This New Testament is also the work of Jay Adams. It omits all the notes and helps present in his earlier work of 1977, The Christian Counselor's New Testament, but prints the exact same text. He claims to take the middle course "between wooden literalness and too much freedom with the text." As the title acknowledges, this translation uses "everyday English throughout."

1981

The Sacred Scriptures

Produced by the Assemblies of Yahweh, this translation was based on the American Standard Version of 1901 and was "the culmination of more than five centuries of translation work." The foundation of this version is its desire to remedy the fact "the Sacred Name of our Heavenly Father Yahweh was removed from the text of the Bible because of a misguided desire to preserve it from desecration by the heathen." It claims to have "restored the Sacred Name and the sacred titles to the English text of the Old Testament as well as returning the Name of Yahshua the Messiah our Redeemer to the text of the New Testament." At the same time, the elimination of "Shakespearean English which is no longer employed in modern usage" was sought for while not resorting "to the modern corrupt slang common in American English."

1982

The Reader's Digest Bible

This is not a new translation but merely a condensation. It was based on the Revised Standard Version. Bruce Metzger served as General Editor and certified that "the work has been thoroughly objective, without bias toward or against any particular set of beliefs." The end result of this condensation is a reduction in the biblical text of forty percent.

New King James Version

This was first presented in 1979 as just the New Testament. Although many translations since the King James Version have claimed to be revising that version in some way, the New King James Version perceives itself to be "a continuation of the labors of the earlier translators, thus unlocking for today's readers the spiritual treasures found especially in the Authorized Version of the Holy Scriptures." Thus it claims to be the fifth major revision of the King James Version, the last one being the 1769 Oxford revision of Benjamin Blayney. A special feature of the New King James Version "is its conformity to the thought flow of the 1611 Bible." A British edition was released a few months after the American edition entitled The Revised Authorised Version.

The initial guidelines followed in translation were:

1. Retain all doctrinal and theological words unless the Greek or Hebrew clearly indicates otherwise.
2. Retain words for items no longer in current use.
3. Correct all departures from the Textus Receptus.
4. Words that have changed meaning since 1611 should be replaced by their modern equivalents.
5. Archaic idioms should be replaced by modern equivalents.
6. Words and expressions that have become vulgar or indelicate in current English usage should be replaced by their proper equivalent.
7. Alter punctuation to conform with that currently used.
8. Change all Elizabethan pronouns, verb forms, and words having "eth" endings to their current equivalent.
9. Attempt to keep King James word order. However, when comprehension or readability is affected transpose or revise sentence structure.
10. Eliminate the inordinate usage of the auxiliary verb "shall." Follow current grammatical style for these changes.
11. Attempt to keep sentences reasonably short without affecting text or meaning.
12. Attempt to use words that avoid misunderstanding.
13. When making corrections use other words already represented by the same Greek or Hebrew word in the King James if possible.
14. Capitalize all personal pronouns referring to deity.
15. Proper names should agree with Old Testament when possible.
16. All obsolete and archaic words as defined by one or more recognized dictionaries should be replaced by

their current equivalents. This applies to phrases and idioms as well.

The executive editor of the project was Arthur Farstad. Over 100 scholars labored seven years under the initiation and sponsorship of Thomas Nelson Publishers. The translation follows the "complete equivalence" principle rather than the "dynamic equivalence" method. Italics to indicate language not in the original languages, but required to complete the sense, were not used in the initial publication of the New Testament in 1979, but were restored in subsequent printings. The Old Testament text follows the Stuttgart edition of *Biblia Hebraica* with reference to the first Bomberg edition, the Septuagint, the Latin Vulgate, the Dead Sea Scrolls, and ancient versions. The New Testament was based on the Received Text with variants of the Alexandrian and Majority Texts noted in footnotes. The footnotes "make no evaluation of readings, but do clearly indicate the manuscript sources of readings which diverge from the traditional text."

1985

New Jerusalem Bible

A revision of the 1966 Jerusalem Bible, this Roman Catholic translation follows its predecessor by being the counterpart of the French Jerusalem Bible. But in this case, the French revision published in 1973. This edition, although likewise translated from the original languages, follows the French only "where the text admits of more than one interpretation."

The Original New Testament

This is a revision by Hugh Schonfield of his earlier translation, The Authentic New Testament.

Tanakh: The Holy Scriptures

Originally published in three stages, this Old Testament was produced by the Jewish Publication Society. It claims to adhere "strictly to the traditional Hebrew text." However, "the entire gamut of biblical interpretation, ancient and modern, Jewish and non-Jewish, has been consulted, and, whenever possible, the results of modern study of the languages and cultures of the ancient near East have been brought to bear on the biblical text." The translators also sought to avoid "obsolete words and phrases and, whenever possible, rendered Hebrew idioms by means of their normal English equivalents."

1986

International Children's Bible

This is a complete edition of the New Century Version first published in 1984 as a New Testament. It claims to be "the first translation of the Holy Scriptures prepared specifically for children." The vocabulary was based on *The Living Word Vocabulary* of 1981. The International Children's Bible claims it was judged "the easiest version for children to comprehend on the literal level" and that it was "the only version that could be comprehended on a third-grade instructional level."

New Life Version

First published in 1969 as The Children's New Testament, this is the completed work of Gleason Ledyard. As the New Testament, this translation uses a limited vocabulary of about 850 words, although words unique to the Old Testament were added. It is claimed that "even educated adults who are familiar with the Scriptures find themselves startled into new insights by is blunt simplicity." The reader should be assured "of an accurate text" which says "what the original languages said."

1987

Easy-to-Read-Version

This translation, from the World Bible Translation Center,

has been "prepared to meet the special needs of the deaf." The translators "worked to convey to their special audience the meaning of the Biblical text in a form that would be simple and natural." It is said to be for those who face "difficulties in reading." It was also "translated from the original languages."

English Version for the Deaf

This version contains the exact text of the Easy-to-Read-Version with a different title affixed.

A Literal Translation of the Bible

This is another work by Jay P. Green that first appeared in The Interlinear Bible. This volume maintains its plan is "to provide every English-reading person with the words of God in their literal richness of expression." It is an attempt to "convey in literal, simple English what God has written for His people."

New Century Version

This is the complete edition of the New Century Version which first appeared as a New Testament in 1984. The original New Testament claimed its purpose was to accurately state "the meaning of Scripture in language that can be clearly understood, even into the next century." The primary concern of the translators was that "the translation be accurate and faithful to the original manuscripts." Some of the translators also worked on other versions including the New King James Version. In addition, "The most recent scholarship and the best available Hebrew and Greek texts have been used, principally the third edition of the United Bible Society's Greek text and the latest edition of the Biblia Hebraica, along with the Septuagint."

1988

Revised New Testament: New American Bible

This Roman Catholic translation of the New Testament is a

revision of the New American Bible of 1970. The purposes of the original translation have been maintained in this revision. The editors have "moved in the direction of a formal-equivalence approach to translation." However, they also "wished to produce a version in English that reflects contemporary American usage." Special attempt has been made to remove gender inclusive language. The Greek text followed was the United Bible Societies' third edition. Nestle's twenty-sixth edition was also consulted. This translation supposedly "does not introduce any changes, expansions, additions to, or subtractions from the text of Scripture."

New Evangelical Translation

This New Testament is produced by God's Word To The Nations Bible Society. A second edition was released in 1992. An American Translation by William Beck was used as a base for this version although the twenty-five scholars who produced it worked "directly from Greek texts." The intention of this translation is to bring "God's Word to the nations." This translation uses the "closet natural equivalent" method of translating. The reading level is "accessible to children without being condescending to adults."

1989

God's New Covenant

This translation of the New Testament, although actually begun in 1957, came to fruition posthumously in 1989. It is the work of a Jewish Christian, Heinz W. Cassirer, who "aimed for a clarity that would be sensitive to every inflection of the original Greek." The translation displays an "attentiveness to Jewish sensibilities." It was based on the Greek editions of Nestle and the United Bible Societies.

Revised English Bible

This is a revision of the New English Bible of 1970. Like its namesake, it is available with the Apocrypha. The claim is made that this is "the most readable and accurate contemporary English translation of the ancient texts available. It is an ecumenical translation, "unencumbered by doctrinal bias," and is supposedly "the most comprehensible and precise English translation of the Bible ever made." The "thou form" of address to God has been abandoned as well as gender exclusive language. The New Testament is based on Nestle's 26th edition.

Jewish New Testament

This version emphasizes that the reason it is different from all other New Testaments is because it expresses the "original and essential Jewishness" of the New Testament. The Jewish New Testament seeks to remove the "centuries-old antisemitic theological biases" inherent in other translations. This is to be accomplished by highlighting the Jewishness of the New Testament cosmetically, culturally and religiously, and theologically. The lone translator of this work is David Stern, a Messianic Jew who now lives in Jerusalem. The translation was primarily based on the United Bible Societies' 3rd edition, and tends toward the "dynamic equivalence" method of translating.

New Revised Standard Version

As its name implies, this is a revision of the Revised Standard Version. The chairman of the Revised Standard Version Bible Committee was Bruce Metzger. It is available with both the Apocryphal and Deuterocanonical books. This revision came about primarily because of "significant advances" in the "discovery and interpretation" of Hebrew and Greek documents. The Old Testament was based on the *'Biblia Hebraica Stuttgartensia* (1977; ed. sec. emendata, 1983)" and corrections adopted were founded on ancient versions. Where none of the versions proved satisfactory, the "best judgement of competent scholars" was relied upon. The New Testament was established on the United Bible Societies' 3rd corrected edition, with "changes to be introduced into the critical apparatus of the forthcoming 4th edition" made available to the translation committee. The translation as a whole was to "continue in the tradition of the King James Bible, but to introduce such changes as are warranted on the basis of accuracy, clarity, euphony, and current English usage." Due to the "danger of linguistic sexism," masculine oriented language has been eliminated as much as possible. Like its predecessor, the New Revised Standard Version "seeks to preserve all that is best in the English Bible as it has been known and used through the years."

1990

The New Translation

This translation includes at the present Romans through Jude and is produced by The Society for The New Translation. The Secretary and Literary Editor is Kenneth Taylor, the translator of The Living Bible. It purports to be "not only accurate in its fresh renderings of the Greek text, but is the easiest of all the versions to read and understand." Gender neutral language is used and deemed "important and helpful." The underlying text is the United Bible Societies' third corrected edition, although it is "eclectic in variations from this base."

Modern King James Version

This is another work by Jay P. Green. Its justification is that "there has been a falling away from the King James Version due to the language difficulties." Some "improvements" to the King James Version include: replacement of archaic language and words that have changed in meaning, modern usage of sentence and word formation, translation of the names of places, and correction of mistranslations. The reader is also informed that "no improvement has been made without referring to the original languages."

1991

Contemporary English Version

Produced by the American Bible Society, this is a translation of just the New Testament. It is declared to be translated "directly from the original Greek," and that "every word, phrase, and clause of the original was carefully studied by the translators." But on the other hand, it was "translated directly from the Greek text published by the United Bible Societies (third edition, corrected, 1983)." Traditional words such as reconciliation, salvation, and sanctification have been changed because "they are not used in everyday English."

21st Century King James Version

This New Testament translation also includes Psalms, Proverbs, and Ecclesiastes, and is labeled volume one in anticipation of the rest of the Old Testament. It is appropriately produced by 21st Century King James Bible Publishers. The Editors profess to be only updating the King James Version and that their work "is not in any way to be thought of as a new translation." This is accomplished by "the elimination of obsolete and archaic words which today are not readily understood by the literate Bible-reading public, and otherwise to adapt Biblical English to accommodate, when necessary, to language changes which have evolved over the course of almost four centuries."

EPILOGUE

Can the continued proliferation of multiplied translations of the Bible be justified? Are further revisions of existing English translations desired or necessary? Has the dissemination of English versions of the Bible reached the point of saturation? Is there a demonstrated need for more, or are any further reasons for new translations just manufactured? Are additional English translations auspicious and beneficial or foreboding and harmful?

The reasons given to justify each translation are myriad and varied. Many aim to update, clarify, improve, correct, or revise the King James Version and other versions due to their imprecise, inaccurate, obsolete, or archaic terminology. Others seek to amplify, expand, explain, or restore the original text. Some claim to be more accurate, faithful, or useful than anything previously available. A few maintain that discoveries of better, older, ancient, or more accurate manuscripts rationalize a new translation. Still some contend that new editions of the Greek New Testament or better modern scholarship justify a new edition if not a new version. But most aspire to render the Bible into modern, contemporary, plain, everyday, natural, basic, understandable, or simple English.

Whether one desires additional revisions and translations or not, we can undoubtedly expect more to come in the future. Regarding existing English translations, we can definitely look for the completion of the Old Testament for any New Testaments that have already been issued. We can also anticipate revisions of existing translations, either superficial and unannounced or substantial and trumpeted. Reissues under new titles will also be forthcoming. More updates of the King James Version are certainly in order as well as new versions in that tradition. Fresh translations can be envisioned based on the recent Majority Greek Text. Further editions of other Greek texts will heighten production of even newer English translations.

In the end, there emerges only three possibilities as to the desires and motives of the translators and publishers of any new or existing translation of the Bible. The first and frequently impassioned reason is the desire to uphold, promote, and disseminate the pure word of God:

> The words of the LORD are pure words: as silver tried in a furnace of earth, purified seven times (Psalm 12:6).

> All scripture is given by inspiration of God, and is profitable for doctrine, for reproof, for correction, for instruction in righteousness (2 Timothy 3:16).

The second and fervently disavowed purpose is to deliberately confuse and deceive the populace by the deceitful corruption of the pure word of God:

> For we are not as many, which corrupt the word of God: but as of sincerity, but as of God, in the sight of God speak we in Christ (2 Corinthians 2:17).

> But have renounced the hidden things of dishonesty, not walking in craftiness, nor handling the word of God deceitfully; but by manifestation of the truth commending ourselves to every man's conscience in the sight of God (2 Corinthians 4:2).

The final and equally denied premise is the avarice and rapacity of those directly responsible for the producing of the pure word of God:

> Perverse disputings of men of corrupt minds, and destitute of the truth, supposing that gain is godliness: from such withdraw thyself (1 Timothy 6:5).

> For the love of money is the root of all evil: which

while some coveted after, they have erred from the faith, and pierced themselves through with many sorrows (1 Timothy 6:10).

After tracing the origin and development of English Bible translations throughout history, it is apparent and unmistakable that something is amiss. Can so many translations, contradicting each other in so many places and in so many ways, each be considered the word of God? Obviously they cannot, for "God is not the author of confusion" (1 Corinthians 14:33a). Although it has not been the intent of this work to analyze and classify any particular translation of the Bible, and the mass of evidence presented has been primarily historical in nature, enough information has been given to enable the reader to make an intelligent decision based on the manner of the translation, the motive of the translators, and the historical significance alone.

APPENDIX

The following is an attempt to comprehensively tabulate all English translations of the Bible since 1611. As the body of this work, the focus of this Appendix is on complete Bibles or separate Old or New Testaments. After the year is given, the complete title is supplied if known. In the case of extremely lengthy or obscure titles, a partial or descriptive title is provided. Unless specified otherwise, each version should be considered a complete Old and New Testament. If the title does not indicate whether the version is a complete Bible or an Old or New Testament, that designation is furnished. The translators names are given, if produced by one or two individuals, but not if by a group or committee since it would be infeasible to do so. Many of these ensuing translations do not appear in the body of the work simply because nothing else is known about them other than the title, year, and translator.

1653 A Paraphrase, and Annotations Upon all the Books of the New Testament; Henry Hammond.

1657 The Dutch Annotations upon the whole Bible; Theodore Haak.

1685 New Testament with a paraphrase and notes; Richard Baxter.

1690 The Holy Bible; Samuel Clarke.

1703 Paraphrase and Commentary on the New Testament; Daniel Whitby.

1718 The New Testament; Cornelius Nary.

1724 The Common translation corrected, with a paraphrase and notes (NT); Edward Wells.

1729 The New Testament in Greek and English; Daniel Mace.

1730 Annotations on the New Testament of Jesus Christ;

Robert Witham.

1730 The New Testament; William Webster.

1745 Primitive New Testament; William Whiston.

1752 Exposition of the New Testament in the form of a Paraphrase; John Guyse.

1755 Explanatory Notes on the New Testament; John Wesley.

1756 Family Expositor, or, a Paraphrase and Version of the New Testament; Philip Doddridge.

1761 An Interpretation of the New Testament; John Heylin.

1764 A new and literal translation of all the books of the Old and New Testament; Anthony Purver.

1764 The New Testament: carefully collated with the Greek, and corrected; Richard Wynne.

1765 A New Translation of the New Testament; Samuel Palmer.

1765 Explanatory Notes upon the Old Testament; John Wesley.

1768 A Liberal Translation of the New Testament; Edward Harwood.

1770 The New Testament or New Covenant of our Lord and Saviour Jesus Christ; John Worsley.

1773 The Universal Family Bible; Henry Southwell.

1774 The Old Testament; Anselm Bayly.

1778 The Bible in Verse; John Fellows.

1791 A Translation of the New Testament; Gilbert Wakefield.

1795 A Translation of the New Testament from the original Greek; Thomas Haweis.

1795 The New Testament; Samuel Clarke and Thomas Pyle.

1796 The New Testament; William Newcome.

1798 A Translation of the New Testament from the Original Greek; Nathaniel Scarlett.

1799 A Revised Translation and Interpretation of the Sacred Scriptures; J.M. Ray.

1808 The Holy Bible containing The Old and New Covenant; Charles Thomson.

1808 The New Testament, in an improved version; Thomas Belsham.

1812 A modern, correct, and close translation of the New Testament; William Williams.

1816 The New Testament; William Thomson.

1817 A new family Bible, and improved version; Benjamin Boothroyd.
1822 The Holy Bible, Hebrew and English (OT); A. Alexander.
1823 The New Testament; Abner Kneeland.
1824 Revised Testament (NT); John Wilkins.
1824 The Holy Bible; J. Watson.
1826 The Sacred Writings of the Apostles and Evangelists of Jesus Christ (NT); Alexander Campbell.
1828 The Gospel of God's Anointed (NT); Alexander Greaves.
1828 The New Testament in the Common Version; John Palfrey.
1833 The Holy Bible; Noah Webster.
1833 A New and Corrected Version of the New Testament; Rodolphus Dickinson.
1834 The Holy Bible; George Townsend.
1835 The Holy Writings of the First Christians (NT) J.M. Caldecott.
1836 The Book of the New Covenant (NT); Granville Penn.
1840 The New Testament; Edgar Taylor.
1841 The Holy Bible; J.T. Conquest.
1842 The Holy Bible; A.C. Kendrick (NT).
1844 The Holy Bible; T.J. Hussey.
1844 The Septuagint version of the Old Testament; Lancelot Brenton.
1848 The New Testament; Jonathan Morgan.
1849 The New Testament; J.W. Etheridge.
1849 The Good News of Our Lord Jesus, the Anointed; Nathan Whiting.
1850 The New Testament; Spencer Cone and William Wyckoff.
1851 The New Testament; James Murdock.
1852 An Exposition of the New Testament; Hezekiah Woodruff.
1853 The Twenty-Four Books of the Holy Scriptures (OT); Isaac Leeser.
1854 The Emphatic New Testament; John Taylor.
1857 The New Testament; John Bengel.
1857 The New Testament; J.A. Giles.
1858 The New Testament, Translated from the Original Greek; Leicester Sawyer.

1858 The Old Testament Scriptures; Alexander Vance.
1860 The Holy Bible; Francis Kenrick.
1861 Jewish School and Family Bible (OT); A. Benisch.
1861 The New Testament; Leonard Thorn.
1862 The Holy Scriptures of the Old Covenant (OT).
1862 A Revised Translation of the New Testament; H. Highton.
1863 The Holy Bible; Robert Young.
1864 An English Version of the New Testament; Herman Heinfetter.
1864 American Bible Union Version (NT).
1864 The Emphatic Diaglott (NT); Benjamin Wilson.
1864 The New Testament; Henry Anderson.
1865 The Holy Bible; Samuel Sharpe.
1865 The Twofold New Testament; Thomas Green.
1867 The Holy Scriptures; Joseph Smith.
1869 The New Testament: Authorized Version Revised; Henry Alford.
1869 The New Testament; George Noyes.
1869 The New Testament; Robert Ainslie.
1870 The Holy Bible; F.W. Gotch (OT), G.A. Jacob (NT).
1870 The New Testament, translated from the purest Greek; J. Bowes.
1873 The School and Children's Bible.
1873 The Story of the Bible; Charles Foster.
1875 The New Testament; John McClellan.
1875 The New Testament; Samuel Davidson.
1876 The Holy Bible; Julia Smith.
1877 Revised English Bible.
1877 The New Testament; John Richter.
1880 The Holy Bible (OT); Hermann Gollancz.
1881 Revised Version.
1881 Jewish Family Bible (OT); Michael Friedlander.
1881 The New Testament Englished; William Crickmer.
1883 The New Testament; Cortes Jackson.
1884 The Englishman's Bible; Thomas Newberry.
1885 The Teaching and Acts of Jesus of Nazareth and His Apostles (NT); W.D. Dillard.
1885 The New Covenant (NT); John Hanson.
1885 A New Translation; John Darby.

1885 A translation of the Old Testament Scriptures from the original Hebrew; Helen Spurrell.

1893 Scriptures, Hebrew and Christian; John Peters and Edward Bartlett.

1892 Biblia Innocentium; John Mackail.

1897 The New Testament Emphasized; Horace Morrow.

1897 The New Dispensation (NT); Robert Weekes.

1898 American Revised Version.

1898 The Woman's Bible.

1901 The Historical New Testament; James Moffatt.

1901 American Standard Version

1901 The Modern American Bible; Frank Ballentine.

1902 Translation of the New Testament from the Original Greek; W.B. Godbey.

1902 The Testament of our Lord (NT); James Cooper and A.J. MacLean.

1902 Twentieth Century New Testament.

1902 The Emphasized Bible; Joseph Rotherham.

1903 The Holy Bible: Marginal Readings Adopted.

1903 The New Testament in Modern Speech; Richard Weymouth.

1903 The Holy Bible in Modern English; Ferrar Fenton.

1904 The Corrected English New Testament; Samuel Lloyd.

1904 The New Testament Revised and Translated; Adolphus Worrell.

1906 The New Testament; Thomas Lindsay.

1907 The Modern Reader's Bible; Richard Moulton.

1908 The Holy Bible for Daily Reading; J.W. Genders.

1909 The University New Testament; S. Townsend Weaver.

1909 The Shorter Bible.

1909 The Bible in Modern English (NT); Frank Ballentine

1910 The Restored New Testament; James Pryse.

1911 The 1911 Tercentenary Commemoration Bible.

1912 The Holy Bible: An Improved Edition.

1913 The Literary Man's New Testament; W.L. Courtney.

1913 The New Testament; Edward Clarke.

1914 The New Covenant (NT); Edward Cunnington.

1914 The New Testament from the Greek text as established by Bible Numerics; Ivan Panin.

1916   The Historical Bible; Charles Kent.
1916   The Twenty-Four Books of the Old Testament; Alexander Harkavy.
1917   The Holy Scriptures According to the Masoretic Text (OT).
1918   The New Testament; Henry Anderson.
1919   The Messages of the Bible; Frank Sanders and Charles Kent.
1919   The Adelphi New Testament; E.E. Cunnington.
1921   A Plain Translation of the New Testament; By a student.
1921   The Shorter Bible.
1922   The Children's Bible; Henry Sherman and Charles Kent.
1922   A Plainer Bible (NT); Frank Ballentine.
1923   Simplified New Testament; D.A. Sommer.
1923   The Riverside New Testament; William Ballantine.
1924   Centenary Translation of the New Testament; Helen Montgomery.
1924   The Everyday Bible; Charles Sheldon.
1924   The Older Children's Bible.
1924   The New Covenant: Labor Determinative Version (NT).
1925   The People's New Covenant (NT); Arthur Overbury.
1926   The Holy Bible: A New Translation (NT); James Moffatt.
1926   Concordant Version (NT); A.E. Knoch.
1926   The Western New Testament; E.E. Cunnington.
1927   The Student's Old Testament; Charles Kent.
1928   The Student's Greek Testament; A. Hamilton.
1928   The Christian's Bible: New Testament; George LeFevre.
1928   The Living Bible; Bolton Hall.
1928   The Authentic Literature of Israel (OT); Elizabeth Czarnomska.
1928   The Cambridge Shorter Bible.
1929   The New Testament in blank verse; George Wolff.
1929   A Homiletical and Exegetical Version of the Bible; Charles MacLean.
1931   The Complete Bible: An American Translation; J.M. Smith and Edgar Goodspeed.
1933   Short Bible; J.M. Smith and Edgar Goodspeed.
1934   The Documents of the New Testament; G.W. Wade.
1934   Old Testament in Colloquial English.

1934 The Child's Story Bible; Catherine Vos.
1935 The Westminster Version of the Sacred Scriptures (NT).
1935 The New Testament; Fernand Faivre.
1936 The West China Union University Version (NT).
1936 The Aldine Bible: The New Testament; M.R. James and Delia Lyttelton.
1936 The Bible Designed to be Read as Living Literature; Ernest Bates.
1937 The New Testament in the Language of the People; Charles B. Williams.
1937 The New Testament of our Lord and Saviour Jesus Christ; Francis Spencer.
1937 The New Testament critically reconstructed and retranslated; William Martin.
1937 The New Testament: A New Translation and Explanation; Johannes Greber.
1938 The Book of Books (NT); R. Mercer Wilson.
1938 The New Testament: A Translation; Edgar Clementson.
1939 The Book of Life (NT); Zed Copp.
1939 The New Testament Shortened; W.K. Clarke.
1940 The Bible (A Condensed Version); Howard Welsch.
1941 The Confraternity Version (NT).
1945 New Testament: A Translation, Harmony and Annotations; Erwin Stringfellow.
1946 Pathways through the Bible (OT); Mortimer Cohen.
1947 The New Testament; George Swann.
1948 The Holy Bible Adapted for Young Christians.
1948 The Letchworth Version in Modern English; T.F. Ford and R.E. Ford.
1949 The Bible in Basic English.
1950 The New Testament of our Messiah and Saviour Yahshua; A.B. Traina.
1950 The Dartmouth Bible.
1950 The Holy Bible for Young Readers (NT); J.W. Mackail.
1951 The Authentic Version (NT).
1951 Bible in Brief; Peter Ross.
1951 The Shorter Oxford Bible.
1951 The New Testament in Modern English; Olaf Norlie.
1952 The New Testament: A New Translation in Plain English;

Charles K. Williams.
1952 Olive Pell Bible; Olive Bible.
1952 The Living Bible; Robert Ballou.
1952 Revised Standard Version.
1953 The New Testament: A New, Independent, Individual Translation; George Moore.
1954 The New Testament Rendered From the Original Greek; James Kleist and Joseph Lilly.
1954 The New Testament in Cadenced Form; Morton Bradley.
1954 The Septuagint Bible (OT); C.A. Muses.
1955 The Authentic New Testament; Hugh Schonfield.
1955 The Holy Bible: A Translation from the Latin Vulgate; Ronald Knox.
1955 The Compact Bible; Margaret Nicholson.
1955 The Clarified New Testament; P.G. Parker.
1956 The Bible for Family Reading; Joseph Gaer and Chester McCown.
1957 The Holy Bible from Ancient Manuscripts; George Lamsa.
1958 The New Testament of our Lord and Savior Jesus Anointed; James Tomanek.
1958 A Beginner's Bible; Margherita Fanchiotti.
1958 The New Testament in Modern English; J.B. Phillips.
1958 The Self-Interpreting; Ashley Johnson.
1959 The Holy Bible: The Berkeley Version in Modern English; Gerrit Verkuyl.
1960 The Children's King James Bible: New Testament; Jay Green.
1960 A Critical Emphatic Paraphrase of the New Testament; Vincent Roth.
1961 The New Testament of Our Lord and Savior Jesus Christ; Fan Noli.
1961 New World Translation.
1961 The New Testament: An Expanded Translation; Kenneth Wuest.
1961 The Jesus People New Testament; Olaf Norlie.
1961 Simplified New Testament in Plain English; Olaf Norlie.
1961 New World Translation.
1962 Teen-age Version; Jay Green.

1962 Modern King James Version; Jay Green.
1962 The Children's Version of the Holy Bible; Jay Green.
1963 The Holy Name Bible; A.B. Traina.
1963 The New Testament in the Language of Today; William Beck.
1965 The Amplified Bible.
1966 Jerusalem Bible.
1966 The Bible in Simplified English.
1966 The Living Scriptures; Jay Green.
1967 Bible for Young Christians (NT); A.M. Cocaqnac and Rosemary Haughton.
1967 New World: The Heart of the New Testament in Plain English; Alan Dale.
1967 New Scofield Reference Bible.
1967 The Christ Emphasis New Testament; Edward Craddock.
1969 The New Testament: A New Translation; William Barclay.
1969 The Children's New Testament; Gleason Ledyard.
1969 Modern Language Bible; Gerrit Verkuyl.
1969 The Bible Reader.
1970 New American Bible.
1970 King James II Version; Jay Green.
1970 New Testament in Shorter Form.
1970 New English Bible.
1970 The Restoration of Original Sacred Name Bible.
1971 New American Standard Bible.
1971 The Living Bible; Kenneth Taylor.
1972 The New Testament in Modern English; J.B. Phillips.
1972 The Bible in Living English; Steven Byington.
1973 A Child's Bible; Anne Edwards and Shirley Steen.
1973 The Translator's New Testament.
1973 Cotton Patch Version (NT); Clarence Jordan.
1973 Common Bible.
1973 The Better Version of the New Testament; Chester Estes.
1974 The New Testament in Everyday English; Don Klingensmith.
1975 The Word Made Fresh; Andrew Edington.
1976 An American Translation; William Beck.
1976 The Concise Jewish Bible (OT); Philip Birnbaum.

1976 Good News Bible.
1977 The Jerusalem Bible (OT); Harold Fisch.
1977 The Christian Counselor's New Testament; Jay Adams.
1977 The Holy Bible for Children; Allan Johsmann.
1978 Holy Name Bible.
1978 New International Version.
1978 Simple English Bible (NT).
1979 The New Testament in Everyday English; Jay Adams.
1980 The Distilled Bible: New Testament; Roy Greenhill.
1981 The Sacred Scriptures.
1981 The Compact Bible (NT); Pat Excel.
1982 The Readers Digest Bible.
1982 The New Testament; Richard Lattimore.
1982 New King James Version.
1984 The New Accurate Translation (NT); Julian Anderson.
1985 Tanakh: The Holy Scriptures (OT).
1985 The Recovery Version (NT).
1985 New Jerusalem Bible.
1985 Original New Testament; Hugh Schonfield.
1986 International Children's Bible.
1986 New Life Version; Gleason Ledyard.
1987 Easy to Read Version.
1987 A Literal Translation of the Bible; Jay Green.
1987 English Version for Deaf.
1987 New Century Version.
1988 Revised New Testament: New American Bible.
1988 New Evangelical Translation.
1988 Christian Community Bible.
1988 The New Testament; Hugo McCord.
1989 God's New Covenant (NT); Heinz Cassirer.
1989 New Revised Standard Version.
1989 Jewish New Testament; David Stern.
1989 Revised English Bible.
1990 The New Translation (NT).
1990 Simplified Living Bible.
1990 Modern King James Version; Jay Green.
1991 21st Century King James Version (NT).
1991 Contemporary English Version (NT).

BIBLIOGRAPHY

Bruce, F.F. *History of the Bible in English,* third edition. New York: Oxford University Press, 1978.

Chamberlin, William J. *Catalogue of English Bible Translations.* Wesport: Greenwood Press, 1991.

Daiches, David. *The King James Version of the English Bible.* Chicago: The University of Chicago, 1941; reprint, Hamden: Archon Books, 1968.

Herbert, A.S. *Historical Catalogue of Printed Editions of the English Bible: 1525-1961.* New York: The American Bible Society, 1968.

Hills, Margaret T., editor. *The English Bible in America.* New York: American Bible Society and The New York Public Library, 1962.

Kenyon, Frederic G. *Our Bible and the Ancient Manuscripts,* revised edition. New York: Harper & Row, Publishers, 1958.

Kubo, Sakae, and Specht, Walter F. *So Many Versions?* revised and enlarged edition. Grand Rapids: Zondervan Publishing House, 1983.

Lewis, Jack P. *The English Bible from KJV to NIV,* second edition. Grand Rapids: Baker Book House, 1991.

McCrum, Robert, Cran, William, and MacNeil, Robert. *The Story of English.* New York: Viking, 1986.

Metzger, Bruce. *The Text of the New Testament: Its Transmission, Corruption, and Restoration,* second edition. New York: Oxford University Press, 1968.

New Catholic Encyclopedia. New York: McGraw-Hill Book Company, 1967.

Penniman, Josiah H. *A Book About the English Bible.* New York: The Macmillan Company, 1919.

Pope, Hugh. *English Versions of the Bible,* revised and amplified edition. St. Louis: B. Herder Book Co., 1952; reprint, Westport: Greenwood Press, 1972.

Price, Ira M. *The Ancestry of Our English Bible,* third revised edition. New York: Harper & Row, Publishers, 1956.

Robinson, H. Wheeler, editor. *The Bible in Its Ancient and English Versions.* Oxford: Claredon Press, 1940; reprint, Westport: Greenwood Press, 1970.

Skilton, John H. "The Translation of the New Testament into English, 1881-1950: Studies in Language and Style." Ph.D. dissertation, University of Pennsylvania, 1961.

The Cambridge History of the Bible. Cambridge: Cambridge University Press, 1963-1970.

The Interpreter's Dictionary of the Bible. Nashville: Abingdon Press, 1962.

Weigle, Luther A. *The English New Testament.* New York: Thomas Nelson and Sons Ltd, 1950.